Family C...
International Cookery Course

Step by Step to Exciting Dishes

Dear Readers,

The Family Circle International Cookery Course quickly became a favourite series in our magazine. So many of you wrote and asked for extra copies that we have decided to publish it in a more permanent form. This book contains many additional recipes from the various countries, as well as full-colour, step-by-step instructions on how to prepare the authentic, favourite national dishes. In some cases, where the foreign ingredients are difficult to obtain, we have used more readily available substitutes. You will delight your family and friends with these dishes. Cook them to bring back happy holiday memories, to give an authentic touch to a party with a theme, or just to conjure up visions of a hot, sunny country on a dull English day.

Bon appetit!

Pamela Scott

Family Circle Cookery Editor

CONTENTS

The Cooking of France

French cooking is famous throughout the world. The French housewife has pride in her cooking, taking great care in the selection and choice of ingredients. Exceptionally good food is found in tiny country inns that may be unsophisticated in other respects.

France is a large wine-producing country and as well as its famous wines, a large proportion of which are exported, each district has its 'vin du pays'. The French housewife makes good use of this local wine in her cookery. Long, slow casserole cooking is traditional and the addition of wine not only gives a delicious flavour, but also has a tenderising effect.

The daily menu is varied and consists of a simple breakfast of warm croissants or rolls and hot coffee, and two main meals. Cheese is served before the sweet course. French pâtisserie is well known and the basis is usually Genoese, choux or puff pastry, with rich fillings and soft icings.

France

Coquilles St. Jacques Bonne Femme

1

3

2

4

SCALLOPS: These delicious shellfish are in season from September to April, but they can be bought quick-frozen most of the year. They are found around the coasts of France, Scotland, and off the east coast of Ireland, where they are dredged off the sandy beds. Scallops are usually opened by the fishmonger, and are displayed on the flat shells. For this recipe, where they are served 'en coquille', that is, in the shell, ask your fishmonger for the deep shells.

THE SAUCE: Scallops are lacking in fat and so are improved by serving in a sauce. Dry cider or white wine is used to flavour the sauce. In Brittany, the province of France where scallops are most plentiful, either cider or Muscadet are used, both in the sauce and for drinking with the dish.

ingredients

For 4 portions:
1½lb potatoes
1oz butter
Milk
Salt and pepper
8 scallops

4 tablespoons dry cider or white wine
2oz mushrooms
1oz margarine
3 rounded teaspoons plain flour
Beaten egg
Sprigs of parsley for garnish

method

1. Cook, sieve and cream potatoes with butter and a little milk. Taste and season with salt and pepper. Clean scallops (or ask the fishmonger to do this). Wash and dry 4 deep shells. Remove scallops from flat shells; slice scallops.

2. Measure ½ pint of milk and the cider into a saucepan. (Liquid may have a slightly curdled appearance, but this will disappear when thickened.) Add scallops and simmer, without boiling, for 8 to 10 minutes, until tender. Wash and slice mushrooms. Place in a saucepan with margarine and cook for 4 minutes without browning. Add flour and cook for 2 minutes. Strain liquid from scallops and gradually blend into mixture. Bring to boil, stirring; cook for 3 minutes. Taste and season with salt and pepper and stir in scallops; cover and keep warm. Prepare a moderate grill.

3. Place potato in a piping bag fitted with a large star tube and pipe around edges of the 4 deep scallop shells; brush lightly with beaten egg and brown under grill.

4. Divide sauce between shells, placing it carefully in the centre of potato in each shell. Garnish with parsley and serve, piping hot, with crusty French bread.

Ratatouille

For 4 portions:

2 large onions
2 cloves of garlic
Salt
2 green peppers
1 red pepper
¾ lb courgettes
½ lb tomatoes
2 tablespoons oil
Pepper

1. Peel and slice onions. Peel cloves of garlic and place on a saucer with a little salt. Using a round-ended knife, rub salt against garlic to crush cloves.

2. Cut each pepper into 8 pieces, removing seeds, cores and white pith. Wash courgettes and cut into ¼ in slices. Place tomatoes in a bowl and cover with boiling water. Leave for 1 minute; drain, peel, then cut into slices.

3. Heat oil in a saucepan and cook onion and garlic for 5 minutes without browning.

4. Cover onions with green and red peppers, then the courgettes and, lastly, the sliced tomatoes; sprinkle well with salt and pepper. Cover saucepan with a tight-fitting lid.

5. Cook over a low heat for 30 to 40 minutes until all vegetables are tender. Turn out into a warmed serving dish and serve hot as a vegetable.

Note: Ratatouille is delicious served cold, as a first course.

Soupe à l'Oignon Gratinée

(Onion Soup)

This delicious soup is probably one of the most well known of the French soups. In France, soups are served before the evening meal, but this substantial soup would make an ideal supper snack on a cold evening.

For 4 portions:

1 lb onions
½ oz butter
1 tablespoon oil
1 oz plain flour
2 beef stock cubes
Salt and pepper
4 slices French bread
2 oz French or Swiss
Gruyère cheese, grated

1. Peel and finely slice onions. Heat butter and oil in a large saucepan; add onions and fry slowly for 8 to 10 minutes, or until golden brown.

2. Stir in flour and cook gently for 1 to 2 minutes. Stir in 2 pints cold water and stock cubes; bring to boil, stirring occasionally, cover and simmer for 10 minutes. Taste and season with some salt and pepper, if necessary.

3. Prepare a hot grill. Toast bread slices and place in base of a warmed, heat-proof soup bowl or 4 individual bowls. Pour soup over, sprinkle bread with grated cheese and place bowl or bowls under grill. Grill for 3 to 5 minutes or until cheese is golden brown.

Salade Niçoise

For 4 or 8 portions:

4 standard eggs
8 firm tomatoes
1 green pepper
1 lettuce
2 sticks of celery
4 spring onions
1 (7oz) can tuna steak
A few black olives

FRENCH DRESSING:

3 tablespoons oil
1 tablespoon tuna liquor
2 tablespoons vinegar
Salt and pepper

1. Hard boil eggs for 10 minutes; crack and leave in cold water to cool. Shell and dry on kitchen paper; cut eggs into quarters.

2. Place tomatoes in a bowl and cover with boiling water. Leave for 1 minute, drain, peell, then cut into quarters.

3. Cut pepper in half lengthwise; discard seeds, core and white pith. Cut into slices and place in a small saucepan. Cover with cold water and bring to boil; drain.

4. Wash and break up lettuce. Wash and slice celery. Wash and trim spring onions. Using scissors, snip the onions (including green parts) into a salad bowl.

5. Drain tuna, reserving 1 tablespoon liquor; break into even-sized pieces and place in salad bowl. Add eggs, tomatoes, green pepper, lettuce, celery and black olives.

6. Mix dressing ingredients together and pour over salad. Stir mixture carefully until coated with dressing. Serve for lunch or as a meal starter.

Tarte à l'Oignon

(Onion Tart)

For 4 to 6 portions:

FILLING:
1 lb onions
1 oz butter
2 standard eggs
¼ pint milk
Salt and pepper
1 oz Gruyère or Cheddar
cheese, grated

PASTRY:
Use 4 oz plain flour (see recipe above)

1. Prepare a moderate oven (375 deg F, Gas Mark 5). Place a 7 in flan ring on a baking sheet.

2. Peel and finely slice onions; fry in butter for about 5 minutes, until deep golden brown. Turn out on to a plate and leave to cool.

3. Beat eggs and milk together in a bowl. Add 1 to 2 level teaspoons salt and a shake of pepper.

4. Make up shortcrust pastry and roll out and line flan ring, as directed in recipe for Quiche Lorraine.

5. Place onions in flan case; strain egg mixture into flan case and sprinkle with grated cheese.

6. Bake in centre of oven for 30 to 35 minutes, until filling is set and pastry is golden brown. Remove flan ring 10 minutes before end of cooking time; place on a warmed serving plate and serve warm.

Quiche Lorraine

(Egg and Bacon Flan)

This is one of the classic dishes from the Lorraine region of France.

For 4 to 6 portions:

PASTRY:	FILLING:
4oz plain flour	*6 rashers streaky bacon*
¼ level teaspoon salt	*2 standard eggs*
1oz margarine	*1 (10 fluid oz) carton single*
1oz lard	*cream*
Cold water to mix	*Salt and pepper*

1. Prepare a moderate oven (375 deg F, Gas Mark 5). Place a 7in flan ring on a baking sheet.

2. Place flour and salt in a bowl. Add fats, cut into small pieces; rub in with the fingertips until mixture resembles fine breadcrumbs. Add about 1 tablespoon of water and mix with a fork to form a firm dough.

3. Turn out on to a floured board and knead lightly; roll out to a circle 2in bigger all around than flan ring. Roll pastry around rolling pin and lift on to flan ring. Gently ease pastry into flan ring. Roll off surplus pastry with a rolling pin across top of flan.

4. Remove rind and bone from bacon; cut bacon into strips. Place bacon in a small frying pan; fry for 2 minutes. Drain and place in flan case.

5. Beat eggs in a bowl; stir in cream and a little salt and pepper, then strain into flan case.

6. Bake in centre of oven for 30 to 35 minutes; remove flan ring 10 minutes before end of cooking time. Serve hot or cold.

Note: ½ pint milk may be used instead of single cream.

Petits Pois à la Française

(French-style Peas)

For 4 portions:

2lb fresh peas	*Butter*
5 lettuce leaves	*1 level teaspoon salt*
6 spring onions	

1. Shell peas. Wash lettuce and onions. Trim onions so that just the bulbs remain.

2. Thickly butter a medium-sized saucepan and place lettuce in saucepan; add peas, onions, 3 tablespoons water and salt, then cover.

3. Bring to boil, cover and cook very slowly for 30 minutes, shaking the pan occasionally. Add more water, if necessary, to prevent burning.

4. Pour into a warmed serving dish and serve immediately.

Chou-Fleur à la Polonaise

(Cauliflower Polonaise)

For 4 portions:

1 medium-sized cauliflower	*1 hard-boiled egg*
1oz butter	*1 level tablespoon chopped*
1oz fresh white	*parsley*
breadcrumbs	

1. Wash cauliflower and cut off any coarse stalk and leaves. Cook whole in fast-boiling, salted water until tender, about 15 minutes. Drain thoroughly and place in a warmed serving dish; keep warm.

2. Melt butter in a frying pan and fry the crumbs until golden brown, stirring continuously; drain on kitchen paper.

3. Chop egg white and sieve egg yolk.

4. Add chopped egg white and parsley to crumbs and stir well to mix; sprinkle over cauliflower. Cover top with sieved egg yolk.

Cassoulet

(Haricot Bean Stew)

The ingredients used in Cassoulet vary in the different regions of France, though all contain haricot beans. The word 'Cassoulet' comes from Cassol d'Issel, which was the clay cooking utensil used in the little town of Issel, near Castelnaudary.

For 5 or 6 portions:

1lb haricot beans	*1lb boned middle neck of*
1 medium-sized onion	*lamb*
2 cloves of garlic	*½lb garlic sausage*
1 level teaspoon salt	*1 large (14oz) can peeled*
½lb piece streaky bacon	*tomatoes*
¼ level teaspoon pepper	*2oz fresh white breadcrumbs*
1lb belly pork, boned	

1. Place haricot beans in a large bowl, cover with water and leave to soak overnight.

2. Peel and slice onion. Peel cloves of garlic and place on a saucer with salt. Using a round-ended knife, rub salt against garlic to crush cloves. Remove rind and bone from bacon; cut bacon into ½in dice. Drain beans; place beans, onion, garlic, pepper and bacon in a large saucepan and cover with water. Bring to boil, cover with a lid and simmer gently for 2 hours.

3. Prepare a cool oven (325 deg F, Gas Mark 3). Remove skin from pork; cut pork and lamb into 1in dice. Cut garlic sausage into ½in slices.

4. Strain beans, reserving ¼ pint stock. Layer beans, meat and contents of can of tomatoes in a large casserole. Arrange garlic sausage on top and pour over reserved stock. Cover casserole and cook in centre of oven for 2 hours or until most of stock has been absorbed. Remove lid, sprinkle with breadcrumbs and cook for 30 to 45 minutes until breadcrumbs are golden brown.

France

Coq au Vin

1

2

3

4

THE CHICKEN: Boiling fowls are traditionally used for this dish, but we have used one of the delicious 'oven ready' birds, which are such good value. If you wish to use a boiling fowl, steam it first for about half an hour. Joint it, as shown (or you could buy chicken joints). If the chicken is frozen, thaw it on a plate for about 8 hours.

GARLIC: This is a popular Continental flavour, but can be omitted from this recipe if you do not like it. It is bought in the form of a bulb, made up of pieces called 'cloves', which can be easily peeled off. Each garlic clove needs crushing; this is easily done if a little kitchen salt is first sprinkled over the clove. Garlic flavour can also be added in the form of garlic salt, which is very convenient to use.

BOUQUET GARNI: This is a small bunch of mixed herbs, used for flavouring. It usually consists of a sprig of parsley, a bay leaf, thyme, peppercorns and, sometimes, a blade of mace. The herbs are tied together in a small piece of muslin. The bouquet garni should be removed before serving.

THE WINE: Wine tenderises meat and gives a good, rich flavour. Use an inexpensive wine for cooking. Your wine merchant will advise on the best value. (A half bottle of wine holds just over half a pint.) One or two tablespoons of brandy can also be added.

ingredients

For 4 portions:
1 chicken (2½ lb drawn
weight)
2oz plain flour
4oz unsmoked streaky
bacon
1 or 2 cloves of garlic
(optional)
Salt
4oz button onions

½ lb small mushrooms
Bouquet garni (1 bay leaf,
thyme, parsley,
12 peppercorns)
1oz butter
1 tablespoon oil
½ pint red wine
½ pint giblet stock
1 rounded teaspoon
tomato purée
1 rounded teaspoon sugar
Pepper

method **1.** Remove giblets and rinse the inside of chicken in cold water; dry thoroughly with kitchen paper. Simmer giblets in water for 1 hour for stock. Prepare a moderate oven (375 deg F, Gas Mark 5). With a large, sharp knife, cut through breastbone, then backbone of chicken, to cut into half.

2. Lay each chicken half flat on a board, and cut off the end of each leg to the first joint, and discard. Halve each chicken half between wing and leg; coat in flour. Remove rind and bone from bacon; cut bacon into ½ in strips.

3. Peel clove (or cloves) of garlic, if used; place on a saucer with a little salt. Using a round-ended knife, rub salt against garlic to crush the clove. Peel onions; wash mushrooms. To make bouquet garni: Place bay leaf, a sprig each of thyme and parsley, and peppercorns in a piece of muslin; fold muslin over and tie with string.

4. Melt butter and oil in a large frying pan and fry chicken portions until brown. Place into a large 4 to 5-pint casserole. Fry bacon and onions until golden brown, and mushrooms for 2 to 3 minutes, without browning. Add to casserole. Stir remaining flour into fat in pan and cook for about 2 minutes, until light brown. Remove from heat, stir in red wine and measured giblet stock, then bring slowly to boil, stirring continuously. Add garlic, 1 level teaspoon salt, tomato purée and sugar. Pour over chicken. Place bouquet garni in casserole, so that the string hangs over the edge of the casserole and the bouquet garni is in the sauce (this makes it easy to remove before serving). Cover and cook in the centre of the oven for 1 hour. Before serving, remove bouquet garni, taste sauce and season with some salt and pepper, if necessary. Serve with peas, carrots and creamed potatoes.

Carottes à la Vichy

(Vichy Carrots)

For 4 portions:

1lb new carrots	*½ level teaspoon salt*
1oz butter	*2 rounded teaspoons*
1 rounded teaspoon sugar	*chopped parsley*

1. Scrape carrots and cut into rings.

2. Place in a saucepan with butter, sugar and salt and heat until butter has melted, stirring continuously. Cover and cook over a low heat, stirring occasionally, until tender, about 20 to 25 minutes.

3. Stir in chopped parsley and pour carrots, with the butter, into a warmed serving dish.

Poulet à la Marengo

(Chicken Marengo)

This dish is said to have been invented for Napoleon by his chef after the famous battle of Marengo.

For 4 portions:

4 chicken joints	*Pinch of sugar*
2 onions	*Salt and pepper*
¼ lb mushrooms	*2 slices white bread*
2 tablespoons oil	*from a large loaf*
1oz plain flour	*Fat for frying*
1 chicken stock cube	*Chopped parsley*
¾ pint boiling water	
2 level teaspoons	
tomato purée	

1. Wipe chicken joints and dry on kitchen paper.

2. Peel and slice onions. Wash and slice mushrooms.

3. Heat oil in a frying pan and fry chicken joints for 3 to 4 minutes until brown. Remove and place on one side. Add onions and fry for 2 to 3 minutes. Stir in the flour.

4. Dissolve the stock cube in the water and add to pan. Bring to boil, stirring. Add tomato purée, sugar and some salt and pepper.

5. Return joints to pan with the mushrooms. Cover with a lid or foil and simmer for 30 minutes or until chicken is tender.

6. Remove crusts from bread and cut each slice into 4 triangles.

7. Heat fat in a pan and fry the triangles of bread until crisp and golden brown. Drain thoroughly on kitchen paper.

8. Arrange chicken in a warmed serving dish; spoon sauce over. Garnish the dish with the triangles of bread and sprinkle with chopped parsley.

Pommes de Terre Anna

(Anna Potatoes)

For 4 portions:

1½ lb old potatoes	*Salt and pepper*
2oz butter	

1. Prepare a moderate oven (375 deg F, Gas Mark 5).

2. Wash, peel and thinly slice potatoes. Wash thoroughly and dry in a clean tea towel or on kitchen paper.

3. Melt butter in a small saucepan.

4. Grease a 6in soufflé dish or casserole and arrange potatoes in layers, adding a little melted butter and salt and pepper between each layer. Cover with a piece of buttered grease-proof paper.

5. Place in centre of oven and bake for 45 minutes. Remove paper and cook for a further 20 to 25 minutes, to brown top.

Mille Feuilles

(Thousand Leaf Pastries)

Makes 8 slices:

1 small (7½ oz) packet frozen puff pastry, just thawed

CREME CHANTILLY:

1 (5 fluid oz) carton double cream	*1 level teaspoon castor sugar*
2 tablespoons milk	*½ teaspoon vanilla essence*
Strawberry jam	
Icing sugar	

1. Prepare a hot oven (450 deg F, Gas Mark 8). Dampen a baking sheet.

2. Roll out pastry and trim to an oblong, 13in by 10in. Place on baking sheet and prick with a fork.

3. Bake on second shelf from top of oven for 10 minutes or until well risen and golden brown. Remove from oven, trim sides and cut into 3 oblongs, each 12in by 3in; place on a wire rack to cool.

4. Place cream, milk, castor sugar and vanilla essence together in a bowl; whisk until stiff. Spread cream on 1 piece of pastry, jam on second piece and sandwich together, jam side uppermost.

5. Place plain piece of pastry on top and gently press pieces of pastry together; dust top with icing sugar.

6. Cut into 8 slices before serving.

Croissants

A typical French breakfast consists of warm croissants, served with piping hot coffee.

Makes 12:

YEAST LIQUID:

1 level teaspoon castor sugar
½ pint, less 4 tablespoons, hand-hot water (110 deg F)

1 level tablespoon dried yeast

DOUGH:

1lb strong plain flour
2 level teaspoons salt
1oz lard

1 standard egg
5oz margarine, at room temperature

EGG GLAZE:

1 small egg
½ level teaspoon castor sugar

2 teaspoons water

1. Dissolve sugar in the water in a small basin; sprinkle on yeast and leave until frothy, about 10 minutes.

2. Place flour and salt in a bowl, add lard, cut into small pieces, and rub in with the fingertips. Beat egg and add, with yeast liquid. Mix to a dough with a wooden spoon.

3. Turn out dough on to a floured board. Knead and stretch dough by folding towards you, then pushing away with the palm of the hand. Give dough a quarter turn and repeat, developing a rocking motion. Knead for about 10 minutes, until dough feels firm and elastic.

4. Roll dough into a long strip, about 20in by 6in, taking care to keep dough an oblong shape.

5. Divide margarine into 3. Use 1 part to dot over the top two-thirds of the dough, leaving a small border. Fold dough by bringing bottom third of dough up to cover middle third and folding top third down. Turn dough, so that fold is on the right. Seal edges by pressing with a rolling pin. Gently roll out dough again to a long, oblong strip and repeat rolling, dotting with remaining 2 portions of margarine, and folding, twice more.

6. Place dough in a greased polythene bag and leave in a refrigerator or cold place for 30 minutes.

7. As before, roll out dough to a long strip, and repeat folding and rolling 3 times more. Place in polythene bag and rest dough in refrigerator or cold place for at least 1 hour. The dough can be stored in a refrigerator for up to 3 days at this stage.

8. Beat egg, sugar and water together.

9. To shape croissants: Roll out dough to an oblong, about 12in by 6in; cut dough in half and roll out halves to 12in circles. Cover each circle with greased polythene and leave for 10 minutes.

10. Cut each circle in half, then each semi-circle into 3, to make 12 triangles, each 6in high with a 6in base. Brush each triangle with egg glaze and roll up loosely, from base to tip. Place on an ungreased baking sheet with tips of triangles underneath, and curve each into a crescent shape. Cover with greased polythene and leave to rise at room temperature for about 30 minutes, until light and puffy.

11. Prepare a hot oven (425 deg F, Gas Mark 7).

12. Remove polythene from croissants, brush with glaze and bake in centre of oven for about 20 minutes, until golden brown. Serve croissants warm.

Note: Alternatively, use fresh yeast: Blend 1oz with measured amount of warm water (omit sugar) and use at once. The margarine used should be the firm, waxy, cheaper type.

Palmiers

(Palm Leaves)

Palmiers are crisp golden-coloured biscuits, which are sold in French pastry shops. In Britain, we usually serve them sandwiched together with jam or whipped cream.

Makes 18:

1 large (13oz) packet frozen puff pastry, just thawed

Castor sugar

1. Prepare a hot oven (425 deg F, Gas Mark 7). Grease 2 baking sheets.

2. Using castor sugar, not flour, roll out pastry and trim to an oblong, 12in by 9in. Mark centre of pastry by placing 9in edges together and lightly pressing fold. Open out and brush lightly with water; sprinkle with castor sugar.

3. Fold 9in edges to meet in centre; brush with water and sprinkle with castor sugar. Fold pastry in half, folded sides together. Cut into 18 (½in) slices and place on baking sheets, leaving room for them to spread sideways.

4. Place 1 baking sheet in centre of oven and bake for 15 minutes; remove and turn palmiers over. Bake for a further 5 minutes until lightly browned. Cool on a wire rack and sprinkle with castor sugar. Repeat process with remaining baking sheet.

France

Gâteau Paris - Brest

1

3

2

4

CHOUX PASTRY: This quick-to-make French pastry is light and crisp. It can be made in advance, if preferred, and stored for 3 to 4 days in a tin.

CREME PATISSIERE: A rich custard filling often used in French pastries. It can be flavoured with praline (as in Paris-Brest), vanilla, liqueur, melted chocolate or strong coffee.

PRALINE: A nut and caramel flavouring. It is usually made with almonds, but it can also be made with hazelnuts. For extra flavour, toast the nuts before adding to the caramel. It can be stored in a screw-topped jar and used for flavouring cakes, creams and icings.

ingredients

For 6 portions:

CHOUX PASTRY:
2oz margarine or butter
4oz plain flour
2 large eggs
1oz flaked almonds

PRALINE:
2oz castor sugar
2oz shelled almonds

CREME PATISSIERE:
2 standard egg yolks
2oz castor sugar
1oz plain flour
½ pint milk
1oz butter
Icing sugar

method

1. Prepare a moderately hot oven (400 deg F, Gas Mark 6). Grease a baking sheet, and mark in 8in circle: place an 8in saucepan lid or plate on baking sheet and sprinkle with flour, then remove lid or plate. Place ½ pint water and margarine or butter in a small saucepan and bring to boil. Remove from heat and stir in flour; beat until smooth. Return to a low heat and cook for a further 2 to 3 minutes, beating continuously with a wooden spoon, until mixture leaves sides of pan. Remove from heat and allow to cool

slightly. Whisk eggs; reserve 2 teaspoons and beat remainder into the mixture, a little at a time.

2. Place mixture in a large piping bag without a tube, and, using the marked circle as a guide, pipe thickly, in a ring, on inside of circle on baking sheet; alternatively, spread in a ring with a spoon. Add 1 teaspoon water to reserved beaten egg, brush over choux ring and sprinkle with flaked almonds. Place in centre of oven and cook for 30 minutes; lower heat of oven to moderate (350 deg F, Gas Mark 4) and cook for a further 30 minutes, until golden brown, well risen and crisp. Remove from oven; immediately, cut in half, horizontally, and place both halves, cut sides uppermost, on baking sheet; remove any soft dough from centre of ring with a teaspoon. Return to oven for about 10 minutes, to dry out. Leave to cool on a wire rack.

3. Lightly grease a baking sheet. Place sugar and 2 table-spoons water in a small saucepan; heat, until sugar has dissolved. Boil rapidly, until an even golden brown. Add almonds; pour quickly on to baking sheet and leave to harden. Place caramel and almonds on a board and cover with a double thickness of foil; tap with a rolling pin, until finely crushed. Alternatively, break into pieces and pulverise in an electric grinder. Place egg yolks and sugar in a basin and beat with a wire whisk, until thick, creamy and pale. Beat in flour and 1 tablespoon of the measured milk. Bring remaining milk to boil; gradually add to egg mixture, beating with a wire whisk. Return to saucepan and bring to boil, stirring continuously, and simmer for 2 minutes. Remove from heat and beat in butter.

4. Leave crème pâtissière to cool, stirring occasionally, then beat in praline. Place crème pâtissière in a large piping bag; pipe into pastry base. Top with other piece of pastry, dredge with icing sugar and place on a serving dish. Serve on the day it is made.

Note: The choux pastry ring may be made in advance and stored in a tin for 3 to 4 days, if desired. Fill gâteau just before serving.

Italy

Minestrone

1

2

3

4

This filling soup from northern Italy can be served as a main meal dish. The ingredients are easy to find in this country and can be varied to suit all tastes. Use ham instead of bacon; add dried haricot beans or fresh vegetables in season, such as broad beans, spinach or baby marrows (zucchini, as they are called in Italy). Rice can be used instead of spaghetti. Italians put basil or marjoram in minestrone; use one of these, instead of mixed dried herbs, if you can.

Parmesan cheese is sprinkled on this soup. It is expensive, but only a small quantity is needed. Buy it ready grated or in the piece with its distinctive black rind. A cheese mill is useful for grating pieces of Parmesan. For a supper party, serve minestrone with rolls and Chianti.

ingredients

For 6 portions:
3 rashers streaky bacon
2 sticks of celery or
1 rounded teaspoon
celery salt
3 carrots
2 medium-sized potatoes
1 or 2 cloves of garlic
(optional)
Salt
1 medium-sized onion
1 small leek

1oz butter
1 rounded tablespoon
tomato purée
2 beef stock cubes
3 pints boiling water
¼ level teaspoon mixed
dried herbs, basil
or marjoram
Pepper
Quarter of a small cabbage
1oz quick-cooking spaghetti
4oz shelled peas
2 level tablespoons cornflour
2oz grated Parmesan cheese

method

1. Remove rind and bone from bacon; cut bacon into ½in strips. Wash celery and cut into ½in slices. Wash and scrape carrots; slice finely. Wash and scrape potatoes; cut into ½in dice. Peel clove (or cloves) of garlic and place on a saucer with a little salt. Using a round-ended knife, rub salt against the garlic to crush the clove. Peel and slice onion. Wash leek; trim off root and any tough outside leaves and discard, then cut leek into ½in rings.

2. Melt butter in a large saucepan and add bacon, celery, carrots, potatoes, garlic, onion and leek. Fry slowly for 5 minutes without browning.

3. Add tomato purée. Dissolve stock cubes in 1 pint of boiling water and add, together with remaining water, mixed dried herbs, basil or marjoram, then 1 level teaspoon of salt and a good shake of pepper. Bring to boil, cover and simmer for 20 minutes.

4. Cut off excess stalk and wash cabbage thoroughly. Discard any tough outside leaves; shred finely. Add spaghetti, peas and cabbage to soup. Bring to boil, cover and simmer for a further 20 minutes. Blend cornflour with a little water and add to saucepan. Bring to boil, stirring, and cook for 1 minute. Serve with grated Parmesan cheese and crusty bread.

Ragù Bolognese

(Bolognaise Sauce)

This well-flavoured, versatile meat sauce can be used in Lasagne, or to fill Cannelloni, or as a sauce for spaghetti. It freezes well, so a large quantity can be made at one time and some of it frozen.

¾ lb stewing beef
¼ lb pie pork
¼ lb chicken or lambs' liver
4oz streaky bacon
1 medium-sized onion
1 stick of celery
1 large carrot
1oz butter
1 tablespoon oil
1 beef stock cube
(optional)

¾ pint boiling water
¼ pint dry white wine
(optional)
1 rounded tablespoon
tomato purée
1 level teaspoon salt
½ level teaspoon pepper
2 level tablespoons
cornflour

1. Cut up beef, pork and liver. Remove rind and bone from bacon; cut bacon into small pieces.

2. Place all the meats together in a saucepan, cover tightly and cook over a low heat for 30 minutes, shaking the pan from time to time.

3. Peel and finely chop onion. Wash and finely chop celery; scrape and finely chop carrot.

4. Remove meat from saucepan, cool slightly, then mince; reserve meat juices in a jug.

5. Heat butter and oil in saucepan in which meat was cooked, add vegetables and cook gently, stirring occasionally, for 10 minutes.

6. Dissolve stock cube, if used, in boiling water, add to vegetables with minced meat, meat juices, wine, if used, or ¼ pint cold water, tomato purée, salt and pepper. Bring to boil, cover and simmer for 1 hour. Blend cornflour to a smooth paste with a little cold water; stir into sauce, return to boil and cook for 3 minutes. Taste and season with more salt and pepper, if necessary. Use Ragù Bolognese for Spaghetti Bolognese and Lasagne Bolognese (see recipes).

Spaghetti Bolognese

(Spaghetti with Meat Sauce)

For 4 portions:
Ragù Bolognese (see recipe)
8oz spaghetti

Knob of butter
3oz to 4oz grated Parmesan
cheese

1. Reheat Ragù Bolognese over a low heat, stirring.

2. Cook spaghetti in a large saucepan of boiling, salted water for 15 minutes, or until just soft when pressed between the fingers. Drain and rinse thoroughly with boiling water.

3. Melt butter in saucepan, return spaghetti to pan and toss until coated.

4. Turn spaghetti out on to a warmed serving dish. Pour sauce over and sprinkle with some Parmesan cheese; serve remainder separately.

Lasagne Bolognese

For 6 to 8 portions:
¾ lb lasagne pasta

2½ oz butter or margarine
2oz plain flour
1 pint milk

Pinch of grated nutmeg
½ level teaspoon salt
Pepper

Ragù Bolognese (see recipe)

2oz grated Parmesan cheese

1. Prepare a moderate oven (350 deg F, Gas Mark 4). Grease a shallow, 3-pint, square or oblong ovenproof dish.

2. Cook lasagne in a large saucepan of boiling, salted water, for 15 to 20 minutes, or as directed on packet. Add pasta, one piece at a time, to prevent it sticking together; stir occasionally. Drain and rinse with cold water. Spread lasagne on kitchen paper to dry.

3. Melt 2oz of the butter or margarine in a saucepan. Add flour and stir over a moderate heat for 2 minutes. Add milk, nutmeg, salt and some pepper. Bring to boil, stirring; cook, stirring continuously, for 3 minutes. Taste and add more salt and pepper, if necessary.

4. Arrange one-third of the lasagne in dish, cover with one-third of the meat sauce, then one-third of the white sauce. Repeat layering twice more, finishing with a layer of white sauce. Sprinkle with cheese and dot with remaining butter. Cook, uncovered, in centre of oven for 30 to 40 minutes. Serve hot.

Note: Lasagne is usually served as a meal starter in Italy; this recipe would then serve 10 portions.

Risotto alla Bolognese

(Risotto Bologna-style)

For 6 portions:
4oz streaky bacon
2oz butter
¾ lb Italian rice

2 chicken stock cubes
1½ pints boiling water
¼ pint dry white wine
(optional)

Ragù Bolognese (see recipe)

Grated Parmesan cheese

1. Remove rind and bone from bacon; cut up bacon.

2. Melt butter in a large saucepan, add bacon and fry for 2 to 3 minutes. Add rice and fry gently, stirring occasionally, for 5 minutes.

3. Dissolve stock cubes in boiling water. Add wine, if used, and about ¼ pint stock to saucepan; stir rice until liquid is absorbed. Continue adding stock and some water, if necessary, about ¼ pint at a time, stirring gently, until rice is tender. Test by pressing a grain between thumb and finger.

4. Add Ragù Bolognese and stir over a moderate heat until mixture comes to the boil. Arrange in a warmed serving dish; sprinkle with Parmesan cheese and serve immediately.

Spaghetti Milanese

(Spaghetti with Tomato Sauce)

For 4 portions:

6oz streaky bacon	Pepper
1 onion	1 level teaspoon castor
2 sticks of celery	sugar
2oz mushrooms	Half a bay leaf
1lb ripe tomatoes	8oz spaghetti
½oz margarine	Knob of butter
½oz plain flour	Grated Parmesan cheese

1. Remove rind and bone from bacon; cut bacon into strips.

2. Peel and chop onion; wash and slice celery and mushrooms. Place tomatoes in a bowl and cover with boiling water. Leave for 1 minute, drain, then peel and quarter.

3. Melt margarine in a medium-sized saucepan. Add onion, bacon, celery and mushrooms and cook for 2 minutes.

4. Add flour and cook for 1 minute. Stir in tomatoes, ¼ pint water, some pepper, sugar and bay leaf. Bring to boil, stirring. Cover and simmer for 30 minutes, stirring occasionally.

5. Cook spaghetti in a large saucepan of boiling, salted water for 15 minutes, or until just soft when pressed between the fingers. Drain and rinse thoroughly in boiling water.

6. Melt butter in saucepan, return spaghetti to pan and toss until coated. Turn out on to a warmed serving dish. Remove bay leaf from sauce and pour sauce over spaghetti. Sprinkle with some cheese, serving the remainder separately.

Note: Spaghetti Milanese is usually served as a meal starter in Italy; this recipe would then serve 6 portions.

Cannelloni di Spinaci

(Cannelloni with Spinach Filling)

For 6 portions:

1 packet (8oz) cannelloni	Salt and pepper
1 large (15oz) can spinach	1½oz butter or margarine
8oz curd cheese	1½oz plain flour
4oz grated Parmesan cheese	1 pint milk

1. Cook cannelloni in plenty of boiling, salted water until just tender, about 10 minutes. Drain and rinse with cold water. Spread out on kitchen paper to dry.

2. Place spinach in a sieve; press with a small saucer to remove as much moisture as possible. Place in a basin, add curd cheese and 3oz of the Parmesan cheese. Season with some salt and pepper and mix well.

3. Prepare a moderate oven (375 deg F, Gas Mark 5). Lightly grease 1 large or 2 small, shallow ovenproof dishes.

4. Place filling in a large piping bag without a piping tube, and pipe mixture into the cannelloni (or fill cannelloni with mixture, using a teaspoon). Arrange filled cannelloni, in a single layer, in dish or dishes.

5. Melt butter or margarine in a saucepan, add flour and stir over a moderate heat for 2 minutes. Add milk and bring

to boil, stirring; cook for 3 minutes. Season with some salt and pepper.

6. Pour sauce over cannelloni and sprinkle with remaining cheese. Cook, uncovered, in centre of oven for 25 to 30 minutes until sauce is bubbling. Serve immediately.

Gnocchi alla Romana

(Semolina Squares Baked with Butter and Cheese)

For 4 portions:

1 pint milk	4oz semolina
1½ teaspoons salt	2 standard eggs
Pinch of grated nutmeg	4oz grated Parmesan cheese
¼ level teaspoon pepper	2oz butter, melted

1. Grease a baking sheet.

2. Place milk in a large saucepan with salt, nutmeg and pepper; bring to boil. Gradually stir in semolina and cook over a moderate heat, stirring continuously, until semolina is very thick, about 3 minutes. Remove from heat.

3. Beat eggs together and add 3oz of the cheese. Stir into semolina; mix well.

4. Spread mixture on to baking sheet, to about ¼in thickness. Smooth top with a palette knife. Leave to cool, then place in a refrigerator until firm, about 1½ hours.

5. Prepare a moderately hot oven (400 deg F, Gas Mark 6). Grease a 2-pint, shallow, ovenproof dish.

6. Cut semolina into 1½in squares and arrange, in layers, in dish. Pour the melted butter over squares; sprinkle with remaining cheese. Bake in centre of oven for 25 to 30 minutes. Serve hot.

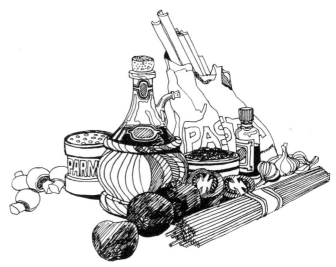

Italy

Scampi alla Livornese

1

3

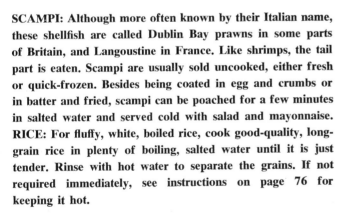

2

SCAMPI: Although more often known by their Italian name, these shellfish are called Dublin Bay prawns in some parts of Britain, and Langoustine in France. Like shrimps, the tail part is eaten. Scampi are usually sold uncooked, either fresh or quick-frozen. Besides being coated in egg and crumbs or in batter and fried, scampi can be poached for a few minutes in salted water and served cold with salad and mayonnaise.
RICE: For fluffy, white, boiled rice, cook good-quality, long-grain rice in plenty of boiling, salted water until it is just tender. Rinse with hot water to separate the grains. If not required immediately, see instructions on page 76 for keeping it hot.

4

ingredients

For 4 portions:
1 or 2 cloves of garlic (optional)
Salt
¾lb ripe tomatoes
1 (3½oz) can tuna steak
½oz margarine
4 bacon rinds
1½ level tablespoons plain flour

¼ pint stock or water
1 level teaspoon tomato purée
Pepper
¼ level teaspoon celery salt
¼ level teaspoon oregano (optional)
3 level teaspoons sugar
8oz peeled scampi
8oz long-grain rice
Chopped parsley

method

1. Peel clove (or cloves) of garlic, if used, and place on a saucer with a little salt. Using a round-ended knife, rub salt against the garlic to crush clove. Place tomatoes in a bowl and cover with boiling water. Leave for 1 minute, drain, then peel. Flake tuna on a plate.

2. Melt margarine in a medium-sized saucepan and fry garlic and bacon rinds for 3 minutes without browning; stir in flour and cook gently for about 2 minutes without browning.

3. Add stock, tomatoes, tomato purée, some pepper, celery salt, oregano, if used, and sugar. Bring to boil, stirring continuously; cook until tomatoes are pulpy. Add scampi; cover and simmer for 15 minutes. Add tuna and heat through for 5 minutes. Taste and season with salt and pepper, if necessary.

4. Cook rice in a large saucepan containing at least 3 pints of boiling, salted water for about 12 minutes. Test by pressing a grain between thumb and finger; drain and rinse with boiling water. Arrange rice on a warmed serving dish, pour scampi sauce over and sprinkle with chopped parsley. Serve piping hot, with crisp green salad.

Note: A large (14oz) can of peeled tomatoes may be used instead of fresh tomatoes. Drain them and place liquor in a measuring jug; make up to ½ pint with water. Omit stock and tomato purée.

Spiedini di Vitello alla Romana

(Veal on Skewers with Cheese and Ham)

For 4 portions:

2 large veal escalopes (8oz to 10oz)
1oz thinly-sliced prosciutto (Parma ham) or 2oz sliced cooked ham
3oz Gruyère cheese
2 (1in-thick) slices from a large white loaf

1oz butter
3 tablespoons oil
8oz Italian or long-grain rice
Pinch of saffron (optional)
2 tablespoons dry vermouth or white wine
1 level tablespoon chopped parsley

1. Flatten veal with a rolling pin; cut each escalope into 6 pieces, each about 3in by 1in.

2. Cut ham into 12 pieces; place a piece on each piece of veal.

3. Cut Gruyère cheese into 12 very thin slices; place a slice on each piece of ham.

4. Remove crusts from bread; cut each slice into 6 cubes.

5. Roll up each slice of veal and thread 3 pieces on to each skewer, with a cube of bread between each roll, and ending with a cube of bread.

6. Remove rack from grill pan; prepare a moderate grill.

7. Place butter and oil in grill pan; place under heat until butter has melted.

8. Add skewers to pan and turn in the fat; grill for about 5 minutes, turning to brown bread and cook meat evenly.

9. Meanwhile, cook rice with saffron, if used, in plenty of boiling, salted water until tender, about 12 minutes. Test by pressing a grain between thumb and finger. Drain and rinse with boiling water. Place on a warmed serving dish.

10. Place skewers on rice and keep hot. Add vermouth or wine and parsley to grill pan and heat under grill. Pour over skewers. Serve immediately with a green salad.

Pizza

For 8 portions:

YEAST LIQUID:

½ level teaspoon castor sugar
¼ pint hand-hot water (110 deg F)

1 level teaspoon dried yeast

DOUGH:

8oz plain flour
1 level teaspoon salt

1 tablespoon oil

TOPPING:

1 large (16oz) can peeled tomatoes
4oz mozzarella or Bel Paese cheese
2oz mushrooms

2oz garlic sausage, sliced
Pinch of oregano or mixed dried herbs
Salt and pepper
Garlic salt (optional)

1. Dissolve sugar in water, sprinkle on yeast and leave until frothy, about 10 minutes. Place flour and salt in a bowl; add yeast liquid and oil and mix to form a soft, but not sticky dough, adding a little more flour, if necessary.

2. Turn out dough on to a floured board and knead and stretch dough, by folding towards you, then pushing away with the palm of the hand. Give dough a quarter turn and repeat, developing a rocking motion. Knead for about 5 minutes, until dough feels firm and elastic.

3. Place dough in a greased polythene bag and leave to rise in a warm place until doubled in size and until dough springs back when pressed with a floured finger, about 45 minutes.

4. Brush a baking sheet, about 14in by 11in, with oil. Prepare a hot oven (450 deg F, Gas Mark 8).

5. Turn out dough on to a floured board and roll out to an oblong, about 12in by 9in. Place on baking sheet and press out with the fingers to cover baking sheet, making dough slightly thicker at the edges.

6. Drain tomatoes, reserving liquor; roughly chop tomatoes and spread over dough. Spoon sufficient tomato liquor over dough to cover it completely. Thinly slice the cheese; arrange evenly over dough. Wash, dry and slice mushrooms; arrange on dough with garlic sausage slices.

7. Sprinkle top with a pinch of oregano or mixed dried herbs, salt, pepper and garlic salt, if used. Brush sausage and mushrooms with a little oil.

8. Bake in centre of oven for 20 to 25 minutes until golden brown and topping is bubbling. Serve hot, cut into oblongs.

Note: Alternatively, use fresh yeast: Blend ¼oz with ¼ pint warm water (omit sugar) and use at once.

Peperonata

For 4 or 5 portions:

2 large onions
1lb ripe tomatoes
2 large green peppers
1 clove of garlic

1 level teaspoon salt
1oz butter or margarine
3 tablespoons oil
Pepper

1. Peel and thinly slice onions. Place tomatoes in a bowl and cover with boiling water. Leave for 1 minute, drain, then peel and roughly chop. Cut peppers in halves lengthwise; discard seeds, core, and white pith. Cut peppers into thin strips lengthwise. Peel clove of garlic and place on a saucer with salt. Using a round-ended knife, rub salt against garlic to crush clove.

2. Heat butter or margarine and oil in a large saucepan. Add onions and tomatoes and cook, uncovered, over a moderate heat, stirring occasionally, until onions are just tender, about 15 minutes. Add green pepper and garlic and continue cooking, stirring occasionally, until peppers are just tender, about 10 minutes. Taste and season with pepper and a little more salt, if necessary. Turn out into a serving dish and serve hot as a vegetable, or cold as a salad with cold meats.

Cassata alla Siciliana

(Sicilian Cassata Cake)

This is a rich cake, layered with a creamy cheese and glacé fruit filling and covered with chocolate icing; in Sicily it is eaten at Christmas and Eastertide, and also at wedding feasts.

For 8 portions:

4oz mixed glacé fruits
(cherries, angelica,
pineapple, etc)
2 tablespoons Strega or
maraschino liqueur or
brandy

8oz cottage cheese
4oz cream cheese
4oz castor sugar
2oz plain chocolate
1 large packet (8) trifle
sponges

CHOCOLATE ICING:

4oz plain chocolate
2oz butter

1 standard egg
6oz icing sugar, sieved

DECORATION:

4 glacé cherries

8 angelica 'leaves'

1. Measure the length of the base of a 2-pint loaf tin; cut a piece of foil the width of this measurement and 12in long. Place foil in tin and press into base and sides firmly; turn extra foil over edges of tin.

2. Chop glacé fruits; place in a basin and add liqueur.

3. Sieve cottage cheese into a bowl. Add cream cheese and sugar; mix well. Chop chocolate finely; add to cheese mixture. Drain fruit, reserving liqueur, and add to cheese; mix well.

4. Split sponge cakes. Line base and sides of tin with sponge cakes, trimming them to fit sides of tin. Reserve 3 pieces of cake for top. Crumble cake trimmings and mix with liqueur from fruit.

5. Place half the cheese mixture in tin; cover with cake-crumb mixture and top with remaining cheese mixture. Press reserved pieces of sponge on to cheese mixture. Fold foil over cake and place in a cold place for several hours. Lift out cake, with foil, and invert on to a serving dish; remove foil.

6. To make icing: Break up chocolate and place with butter in a dry basin over a saucepan of hot, but not boiling, water; stir occasionally, until melted.

7. Beat egg and mix into melted chocolate. Remove basin from saucepan. Add sieved icing sugar and beat until smooth.

8. Quickly spread icing over top and sides of cake.

9. Cut cherries in halves, and arrange 4 halves down each side of cake. Place an angelica 'leaf' on the outside of each cherry. Keep cake cool until served.

Granita di Caffè

(Coffee Water Ice)

For 8 portions:

6oz castor sugar
2 rounded tablespoons
instant coffee

¾ pint boiling water

1. Turn refrigerator to coldest setting.

2. Place sugar and ½ pint cold water in a saucepan, stir over a moderate heat until sugar has dissolved and bring to boil; boil rapidly for 5 minutes, without stirring.

3. Dissolve coffee in boiling water. Add to sugar syrup and mix well; leave until cool.

4. Pour into 2 ice trays and freeze for 1 to 1½ hours.

5. When ice has frozen around sides to 1in thickness, turn out into a bowl, chilled if possible, and whisk until mixture becomes paler in colour and of a fine, even texture.

6. Return to trays and freeze for a further three-quarters to 1 hour. Again whisk until mixture is light and smooth. Return to trays and freeze until firm.

7. Return refrigerator to normal setting and keep water ice in ice-making compartment, until served.

Pesche Ripiene

(Baked Stuffed Peaches)

For 4 portions:

3 macaroons
4 ripe peaches
Butter

2 level tablespoons castor
sugar
1 egg yolk

1. Prepare a moderate oven (350 deg F, Gas Mark 4).

2. Crush macaroons, in a paper bag, with a rolling pin; place crumbs in a basin.

3. Place peaches in a bowl, cover with boiling water and leave for 1 minute; remove skins. Cut peaches in halves; remove stones. Scoop out a little of the peach pulp with a teaspoon, to make a larger cavity; add pulp to crushed macaroons. Place peaches, rounded sides downwards, in an ovenproof dish.

4. Cream 1oz butter and sugar together; beat in egg yolk and crushed macaroons. Pile mixture into peach halves. Dot filling with a little extra butter and bake peaches in centre of oven for about 30 minutes. Serve hot or cold with cream.

Italy

Cassata Gelata

1

2

3

4

Ice cream is made from flavoured custard. Ideally, the custard should be made with cream and egg yolks, in the proportion of 4 egg yolks to ½ pint cream. However, as this mixture is very expensive and rich, a cheaper ice cream can be made with milk and custard powder, with cream or evaporated milk added.

ingredients

For 8 portions:
CHOCOLATE
ICE CREAM:

1 level tablespoon custard powder
1 level tablespoon castor sugar
1 level teaspoon cocoa
½ pint milk
2oz plain chocolate
1 small can evaporated milk

TUTTI FRUTTI
ICE CREAM:

1 level tablespoon custard powder
1 level tablespoon castor sugar
½ pint milk
1 tablespoon maraschino cherry syrup
1 teaspoon almond essence
Pink food colouring
1 (5 fluid oz) carton double cream
½oz seedless raisins
½oz angelica
1oz maraschino cherries

method

1. Turn the refrigerator to coldest setting. To make chocolate ice cream: Blend custard powder, sugar and cocoa in a basin with a little cold milk. Boil remaining milk, pour on to blended custard powder and return to pan; bring to boil, stirring. Remove from heat, add chocolate, broken into small pieces, and stir until melted. Cover with a piece of dampened greaseproof paper, wet side downwards, and place in a bowl of cold water to cool. Meanwhile, make cherry custard for tutti frutti ice cream: Make custard, using custard powder, sugar and milk. Remove from heat, add cherry syrup and almond essence and tint mixture pink. Cover and cool, like chocolate ice cream. To complete chocolate ice cream: Whisk evaporated milk until thick and fold in cooled chocolate custard. Pour into a freezing tray or plastic tray and leave in the ice-making compartment until partially set, about 1 to 1½ hours. Whisk double cream lightly and fold in the cooled cherry custard. Pour into a freezing tray or plastic tray and leave in the ice-making compartment until partially set, about 1 to 1½ hours. Place raisins and angelica in a basin, cover with boiling water and leave for 3 minutes; drain. Coarsely chop raisins, angelica and cherries.

2. Remove chocolate ice cream from refrigerator, scrape into a chilled bowl and whisk until smooth. Pour into a chilled 1½-pint basin, and return to ice-making compartment. Remove cherry ice cream, scrape into a chilled bowl and whisk until smooth. Mix in fruit. Return to tray and ice-making compartment, but do not allow to freeze solid.

3. When chocolate ice cream is half set, remove from refrigerator and, using a round-ended knife, draw ice cream up the side of the basin, leaving a hollow centre. Return to ice-making compartment until firm.

4. Lightly press tutti frutti ice cream into centre of chocolate ice cream; return to ice-making compartment and re-freeze for 1 hour or until firm. Turn refrigerator back to normal setting. To serve: Dip basin into very hot water and turn out cassata on to a serving dish. Serve with wafers.

Note: If the ice-making compartment of your refrigerator is too shallow for a pudding basin, a pie dish, loaf tin or plastic tray (1½-pint capacity) can be used.

Panettone

This popular yeast cake is eaten for breakfast in Italy, but is also delicious as a tea bread, cut into narrow wedges and buttered.

YEAST LIQUID:

1 level teaspoon castor sugar	*1 level tablespoon dried yeast*
¼ pint hand-hot water (110 deg F)	

DOUGH:

3 egg yolks	*14oz strong plain flour*
½ teaspoon vanilla essence	*4oz butter, softened*
1 level teaspoon grated lemon rind	*2oz sultanas*
1 level teaspoon salt	*2oz seedless raisins*
2oz castor sugar	*2oz cut mixed peel*

1oz butter, melted

1. Dissolve 1 teaspoon sugar in the water, sprinkle on yeast and leave until frothy, about 10 minutes.

2. Beat egg yolks together in a bowl; add yeast liquid, vanilla essence, lemon rind, salt and 2oz sugar. Beat in about 8oz of the flour. Gradually beat in softened butter, about 1oz at a time. Beat in remaining 6oz of the flour.

3. Turn out dough on to a floured board. Knead and stretch dough by folding towards you, then pushing away with the palm of the hand. Give dough a quarter turn and repeat, developing a rocking motion. Knead for about 10 minutes, until dough feels firm and elastic.

4. Place dough in a lightly-floured bowl or saucepan, cover with greased polythene or a saucepan lid, and leave to rise in a warm place, until dough is doubled in size and springs back when pressed with a floured finger, about 1 hour. Grease a deep, round, 7in cake tin.

5. Turn out dough on to a floured board; add sultanas, raisins and peel, and knead until fruit is well mixed into dough. Form into a ball and place in cake tin. Cover with greased polythene and leave to rise in a warm place until doubled in size, about 45 minutes.

6. Prepare a moderately hot oven (400 deg F, Gas Mark 6).

7. Remove polythene from tin and mark a cross on top of dough with a sharp knife. Brush top with melted butter. Bake in centre of oven for 20 minutes. Reduce oven temperature to moderate (350 deg F, Gas Mark 4); brush Panettone again with butter and continue cooking for a further 40 to 45 minutes, brushing once more with melted butter about 15 minutes before the end of the cooking time.

8. Remove from oven, turn out on to a wire rack and brush top and sides with remaining butter; leave to cool. Serve, cut into thin wedges.

Note: Alternatively, use fresh yeast: Blend 1oz with ¼ pint warm water (omit 1 level teaspoon sugar) and use at once.

Zabaglione

For each portion:

1 egg yolk	*1 tablespoon marsala*
1 rounded teaspoon castor sugar	*or sherry*

1. Place a deep bowl over a saucepan of hot, but not boiling, water.

2. Add egg yolk, sugar and marsala or sherry and beat with a rotary whisk until the mixture has trebled in bulk. Pour into small glasses and serve immediately. Serve with crisp sweet biscuits.

Note: Fresh orange juice can be substituted for wine, but add a large pinch of grated orange rind for each portion.

Cenci alla Fiorentina
(Deep-fried Sweet Pastry)

These light, deep-fried pastry 'knots' are a speciality of Lucca, a town in the Tuscany region of Italy. Its inhabitants seem to have an especially sweet tooth, as several well known cakes and desserts come from this region. Lucca is also famous for its olive oil, sometimes called the finest in Italy.

Makes 48:

8oz plain flour	*2 standard egg yolks*
¼ level teaspoon salt	*1 dessertspoon*
Icing sugar	*rum or orange juice*
2 standard eggs	*Oil or lard for deep frying*

1. Sift flour, salt and 1 level tablespoon icing sugar into a bowl.

2. Beat eggs, egg yolks and rum or orange juice together. Make a 'well' in centre of flour and add egg mixture. Mix with a wooden spoon or with the hands.

3. Turn out on to a lightly floured board. Knead and stretch dough by folding towards you, then pushing away with the palm of the hand. Give dough a quarter turn and repeat, developing a rocking motion. Knead for about 10 minutes until dough feels firm and elastic and no longer sticky.

4. Place dough in a polythene bag or wrap in foil. Leave in refrigerator for at least 1 hour.

5. Cut dough into quarters. Roll out each piece on a lightly floured board and trim to a 6in square. The dough should be very thin. Using a pastry wheel or sharp knife, cut into strips, 6in long and ½in wide. Tie the strips loosely into 'knots'.

6. Heat a pan of oil or lard to 370 deg F, or until a 1in cube of day-old bread browns in 40 seconds. Fry 4 or 5 knots at a time for 1 to 2 minutes until golden brown. Using a draining spoon, remove knots and drain on crumpled kitchen paper. Keep warm while remainder are being fried. Pile on to a warmed serving dish and dredge with icing sugar. Serve with coffee.

The Cooking of Spain and Portugal

Spain is particularly well known for fish, shellfish, red and green peppers, onions and tomatoes, all of which are frequently used in Spanish dishes. There is little beef served, but some delicious veal and chicken dishes are cooked with well-flavoured sauces. As with most Mediterranean countries, the different regions are noted for their various specialities: the Basque and Galicia regions for fish and shellfish, Asturias for bean stews and cider, Andalusia for gazpacho and the Levante for its marvellous rice dishes. Portugal has a long coastline on the Atlantic ocean, and a great variety of fish, such as plaice, cod, sardines, sea bream, tunny fish—octopus, too—are caught along the coast. Salted cod is popular and is found in many Portuguese fish recipes. Fruit, olives, tomatoes and the grapes, which produce the famous Port, are plentiful.

Spain

Pastel de Tortillas Especial (Special Omelet Cake)

3

4

1

2

TORTILLAS are thick and flat, unlike the rolled French omelets. For cooking, use a thick frying pan. The filling is first cooked in oil in the pan, added to beaten eggs, then returned to the pan and cooked slowly. This Special Omelet Cake is an ideal way of serving omelets for four; it is served, cut into wedges, like a cake, so that each person tastes all the fillings.

ingredients

For 4 portions:
TOMATO SAUCE:
1 small onion
A few celery leaves
or celery salt
½oz margarine
A few bacon rinds
¾lb ripe tomatoes
¼ pint stock or water
Salt and pepper
1 level teaspoon sugar
1 rounded teaspoon
tomato purée (optional)
1 level tablespoon cornflour

FILLINGS:
¼lb cooked mixed
vegetables
2oz mushrooms, sliced
and fried
2oz fresh, frozen or
canned prawns
2 medium-sized new
potatoes, sliced and fried
1 small onion, sliced
and fried
1 level tablespoon
chopped parsley

OMELETS:
8 standard eggs
Salt

Olive oil

method 1. Make tomato sauce: Peel and roughly chop onion. Wash celery leaves. Melt margarine in a small saucepan; add onion, celery leaves and bacon rinds and fry for 3 minutes. Roughly chop tomatoes and add to saucepan with stock, some salt and pepper, sugar and tomato purée, if used. Bring to boil, cover and simmer for 15 minutes. Rub through a sieve, or place in goblet of an electric liquidiser, discard bacon rinds; blend until mixture is smooth, then strain. Rinse saucepan, place cornflour in saucepan, and blend with 1 tablespoon cold water. Add tomato mixture and bring to boil, stirring; simmer for 1 minute. Taste and add some celery salt, if used, and more salt and pepper if necessary.

Make omelets: Break 2 eggs and place, with ¼ level teaspoon salt, into each of 4 individual basins. Beat with a fork until just mixed and add 1 filling to each basin; add parsley to mushroom filling. Heat a little oil slowly in a small, 6in omelet or frying pan, swirl to coat pan, then pour in egg mixture from 1 basin. Cook slowly until underside is golden brown and centre is set.

2. Quickly flip omelet over with a fish slice. Cook over moderate heat until brown.

3. Slide omelet on to a warmed serving dish; keep warm. Make the remaining 3 omelets in the same way and pile them on top of one another on the serving dish to form 'cake'.

4. Reheat the tomato sauce, if necessary; pour over omelet cake and serve immediately, with green salad.

Gazpacho

Gazpacho originates from the fertile Andalusian region, which is an area south of Madrid. The farm workers in Andalusia have gazpacho as a midday meal, and it is prepared in, and eaten from, the same bowl. Outside Spain, it is usually served as a soup.

For 4 portions:

1½ lb ripe tomatoes	Half a cucumber
1 green pepper	1 small (10 fluid oz) can
4 slices white bread from	tomato juice
a large loaf	1 tablespoon tarragon
1 clove of garlic	vinegar
½ level teaspoon salt	2 tablespoons oil
1 small onion	

1. Place tomatoes in a bowl and cover with boiling water. Leave for 1 minute, drain, then peel. Reserve 3 tomatoes for garnish; chop remainder.

2. Cut green pepper in half lengthwise; discard core, seeds and white pith, then finely chop pepper. Reserve half of chopped pepper for garnish.

3. Remove crust from 2 slices of bread; place bread in a bowl and cover with cold water. Leave for 5 minutes to soak; squeeze out water.

4. Peel clove of garlic and place on a saucer with salt. Using a round-ended knife, rub salt against garlic to crush clove. Peel and grate onion. Finely chop cucumber; reserve half of chopped cucumber for garnish.

5. Sieve tomatoes, cucumber, pepper, onion and bread into a bowl. Add tomato juice, vinegar and oil; mix well together. Place in a soup tureen and keep cool until served.

6. Prepare a hot grill; toast remaining 2 slices of bread and cut into cubes. Discard seeds from reserved tomatoes and dice. Place tomatoes, cubed toast and reserved chopped pepper and cucumber in small bowls. Serve with soup.

Note: If an electric liquidiser is available, place all prepared soup ingredients, except tomato juice, in liquidiser goblet and run machine until mixture is smooth. Sieve soup into a bowl and mix in tomato juice.

Mussels in Tomato Sauce

For 3 or 4 portions:

1 quart fresh mussels	1 large (14oz) can peeled
2 cloves of garlic	tomatoes
Salt	Pepper

1. Discard any mussels that do not shut when tapped, as they are probably dead. Scrub shells well and scrape off any barnacles and weeds. Wash thoroughly to remove sand.

2. Peel cloves of garlic and place on a saucer with a little salt. Using a round-ended knife, rub salt against garlic to crush cloves.

3. Sieve tomatoes into a small saucepan. Add garlic and a little salt and pepper; bring to boil and simmer for about 6 minutes.

4. Place mussels in a saucepan, cover them with a cloth and steam them over a low heat until the shells open. Remove 'beard' with a sharp knife and discard one side of shell from each mussel.

5. Place mussels in a shallow dish, pour sauce over and serve, hot or cold.

Ensalada Madrileña

(Madrid Salad)

In Spain, salad is usually served as a first course; it may also be served alone or with slices of ham.

For 4 portions:

1 standard egg	2oz black olives
3 tomatoes	1 (4¼oz) can sardines in
1 lettuce	olive oil

DRESSING:

1 tablespoon tarragon or	2 tablespoons oil
wine vinegar	½ level teaspoon salt

1. Hard boil egg for 10 minutes; crack and leave to cool in cold water, then shell and dry on kitchen paper.

2. Place tomatoes in a bowl and cover with boiling water. Leave for 1 minute, drain, then peel. Chop 2 tomatoes; reserve 1 tomato for garnish.

3. Remove and discard outer leaves from lettuce; wash the lettuce well, then shred. Remove stones from olives.

4. Drain oil from can of sardines into a bowl, add vinegar, oil and salt; mix well together. Chop sardines.

5. Add chopped tomatoes, chopped sardines, olives and lettuce to bowl; stir carefully until well mixed.

6. Arrange salad on a shallow serving dish. Slice egg and reserved tomato; place slices of tomato and egg alternately down the centre of salad.

Paella

(pictured on front cover)

Paella is the best known of Spanish dishes. The ingredients used in paella vary from province to province, but the main ingredients are fish and shell fish, which are abundant around the coast of Spain. Traditionally, paella is cooked in the two-handled, shallow, iron pan from which it takes its name.

For 6 portions:

1 small chicken (about 2lb	1 tablespoon oil
drawn weight)	8oz long-grain rice
¼lb lean pork	Pinch of saffron
1 onion	1 (8oz) can cocktail
1 red pepper	sausages
1 green pepper	½ level teaspoon paprika
2 tomatoes	Pepper
2 cloves of garlic	4oz peeled prawns
Salt	1 small (¼lb) pack
4oz white fish fillet	frozen peas
12 mussels	

1. Cut chicken into even-sized pieces. Place giblets in a saucepan, cover with water and bring to boil. Cover with a lid and simmer for about 1 hour to make stock; strain into a measuring jug. Make up to 1½ pints with water.

2. Cut pork into ½in cubes. Peel and chop onion. Cut peppers in halves lengthwise; discard core, seeds and white pith, then slice peppers. Place tomatoes in a bowl and cover with boiling water. Leave for 1 minute, drain, then peel and chop. Peel cloves of garlic and place on a saucer with a little salt. Using a round-ended knife, rub salt against garlic to crush cloves. Cut fish into dice.

3. Discard any mussels that do not shut when tapped, as they are probably dead. Scrub mussel shells well and scrape to remove barnacles and weeds. Wash thoroughly to remove sand. Place in a saucepan, cover mussels with a cloth and steam them over a low heat until the shells open. Remove 'beard' from each with a sharp knife.

4. Heat oil in a large frying pan. Add chicken, pork, onion and garlic and fry for 5 to 6 minutes.

5. Stir in rice and cook for 1 to 2 minutes, to absorb fat. Add stock, saffron, fish, peppers, cocktail sausages, tomatoes, paprika and a little salt and pepper. Bring to boil and simmer for 15 minutes, stirring occasionally.

6. Add prawns, peas and mussels to pan; add extra water, if necessary. Cook for a further 5 to 6 minutes, or until rice is tender. (The rice should be moist, but not wet.)

7. Place paella in a warmed serving dish and serve.

Tortilla de Patata a la Española

(Spanish Potato Omelet)

This originates from Castile and is one of the many types of tortilla which are made in Spain.

For 2 portions:

3 small potatoes	2 tablespoons oil
1 medium-sized onion	4 eggs
4 rashers streaky bacon	Salt and pepper

1. Peel, wash and thinly slice potatoes. Peel and finely chop onion. Remove rind and bone from bacon; cut bacon into small pieces.

2. Heat oil in a small frying pan and add potato slices, onion and bacon. Cook gently until potatoes are tender.

3. Break eggs into a bowl and beat lightly. Add some salt and pepper.

4. Pour eggs into frying pan and stir once or twice. Cook gently for 3 to 4 minutes until just set. Place under a medium grill for 1 minute.

5. Slip on to a warmed plate; do not fold. Cut in half to serve 2 portions.

Cordero a la Chilindrón

(Lamb with Red Peppers and Tomatoes)

For 4 portions:

1½lb boned middle neck of	1 clove of garlic
lamb	1½ level teaspoons salt
3 red peppers	1oz butter
1 onion	1 tablespoon oil
½lb tomatoes	½ level teaspoon pepper
3oz lean ham	

1. Cut lamb into 1in cubes. Cut peppers into halves lengthwise; discard core, seeds and white pith. Slice peppers and place in a small saucepan. Cover with cold water, bring to boil and simmer for 5 minutes; drain.

2. Peel and chop onion. Place tomatoes in a bowl; cover with boiling water. Leave for 1 minute, drain, then peel and chop. Cut ham into strips. Peel clove of garlic and place on a saucer with salt. Using a round-ended knife, rub salt against garlic to crush clove.

3. Heat butter and oil in a large saucepan; fry lamb and garlic for 2 to 3 minutes. Add ham, onion, tomatoes, red peppers, pepper and 2 tablespoons water. Cover tightly and cook very slowly for 1 hour or until meat is tender.

4. Place on a warmed serving dish and serve with boiled rice.

Spain

Bacalao Andaluz (Andalusian Cod Steaks)

2

1

4

3

COD STEAKS: Choose fish that looks firm and white. Frozen cod steaks could be used; thaw them slowly before adding to the sauce in the dish.

WINE: Stock or water could be substituted for the wine in this recipe. For a special occasion, however, the addition of wine puts this dish into the gourmet class. Use a dry, white wine, such as Spanish Chablis or Graves, or an inexpensive, branded vin ordinaire.

ingredients

4 cod steaks
TOPPING:
1 small onion
2oz mushrooms
1 small green pepper
2 tomatoes
1oz white bread
(without crusts)
1 tablespoon olive oil
1 level tablespoon
chopped parsley

For 4 portions:
1 clove of garlic
Salt
½oz margarine
½oz plain flour
4 tablespoons dry white
wine
White pepper

method

1. Prepare a moderately hot oven (400 deg F, Gas Mark 6). Peel clove of garlic and place on a plate with ½ level teaspoon salt. Using a round-ended knife, rub salt against garlic to crush clove. Melt margarine in a saucepan, stir in garlic and flour and cook gently for about 2 minutes without browning. Add wine and 4 tablespoons water; bring to boil, stirring continuously, and simmer for 2 minutes. Add ¼ level teaspoon white pepper. Pour into a shallow ovenproof dish. Wash cod steaks, dry on kitchen paper and place in dish.

2. Peel and slice onion. Wash and slice mushrooms. Cut green pepper in half lengthwise, discard seeds, core and white pith; cut into strips. Place tomatoes in a bowl and cover with boiling water. Leave for 1 minute, then drain, peel and roughly chop.

3. Using the coarse side of a grater, grate bread to make crumbs (if bread is very fresh, cut into small cubes). Heat oil in a small saucepan, add onion and fry until soft; add mushrooms and green pepper and continue cooking for a few minutes. Stir in breadcrumbs, tomatoes, ¼ level teaspoon salt, a shake of pepper and parsley.

4. Spread topping over cod steaks. Cover with a piece of greased greaseproof paper and bake in the centre of oven for 25 to 30 minutes. Remove paper and serve hot.

Almôndegas

(Meatballs with Tomatoes)

For 4 portions:

1 clove of garlic	½ level teaspoon pepper
1 level teaspoon salt	1 standard egg
4 rashers streaky bacon	Flour
½ oz margarine	1 medium-sized onion
1lb minced beef	6 tomatoes
2 level tablespoons chopped parsley	1 level tablespoon tomato purée

1. Peel clove of garlic and place on a saucer with salt. Using a round-ended knife, rub salt against garlic to crush clove.

2. Remove rind and bone from bacon; cut bacon into small pieces. Melt margarine in a large saucepan, add bacon and fry until crisp. Place bacon, beef, garlic, 1 level tablespoon chopped parsley and pepper in a bowl. Beat egg in a small basin, add to meat mixture and mix well; shape into 20 small balls and lightly coat in flour.

3. Peel and finely chop onion. Place tomatoes in a bowl and cover with boiling water. Leave for 1 minute, drain, then peel and chop.

4. Add onion to saucepan and fry until golden brown. Add tomatoes, tomato purée, 1 level tablespoon chopped parsley and 3 tablespoons water; bring to boil. Add meatballs, cover and simmer for 30 to 40 minutes, stirring occasionally.

5. Place meatballs on a warmed serving dish and pour sauce over. Serve with boiled rice (see page 76).

Sonhos

A favourite sweet dish, served in the Portuguese provinces.

For 3 or 4 portions:

1oz margarine or butter	Oil or lard for deep frying
2oz plain flour	2oz castor sugar
1 large egg	1 level teaspoon cinnamon

1. Place ¼ pint water and margarine or butter in a small saucepan and bring to boil. Remove from heat and stir in flour; beat well.

2. Return to a low heat and cook for a further 2 to 3 minutes, beating continuously with a wooden spoon, until mixture leaves sides of pan.

3. Remove from heat and allow to cool slightly. Whisk egg and beat into the mixture, a little at a time.

4. Heat a pan of oil or lard to 370 deg F, or until a 1in cube of day-old bread browns in 40 seconds. Place mixture in a piping bag fitted with a ½in plain tube and pipe 2in lengths into hot fat. Cook for 5 minutes, until well risen and golden brown; drain thoroughly on kitchen paper.

5. Place sugar and cinnamon in a paper bag and shake gently to mix. Place sonhos in bag, a few at a time, and shake gently to coat. Serve immediately.

Flan de Naranja

(Orange Caramel Custard)

For 4 portions:

CARAMEL:

2oz granulated sugar

CUSTARD:

1 large orange	3 large or 4 standard eggs
¾ pint milk	2oz castor sugar

1. Prepare a very cool oven (275 deg F, Gas Mark 1). Half fill a roasting tin with warm water.

2. Warm a 1¼-pint soufflé dish. Prepare the caramel: Place sugar and 2 tablespoons water in a thick saucepan and heat slowly, until sugar has dissolved; boil steadily, without stirring, until sugar turns a deep golden brown. Pour into the warmed dish and leave for 2 minutes to set; place dish in the roasting tin.

3. Scrub orange. Using a small, sharp knife or potato peeler, remove rind from orange, taking care not to include any white pith. Place milk and orange rind in a saucepan and bring to boil slowly. Gently simmer for 5 minutes.

4. Beat eggs and castor sugar together in a basin. Add milk mixture gradually and beat lightly.

5. Strain the egg and milk mixture on to the caramel. Place roasting tin, containing dish, in the centre of oven and cook for 1 hour or until custard is set and lightly browned on top. Remove dish from roasting tin and leave until custard is quite cold, about 3 hours. Loosen edge of custard by gently pulling towards centre with the fingers; invert on to a serving plate.

6. Remove pith from orange with a sharp or serrated knife; divide orange into segments and arrange around base of caramel custard.

Spanish Chocolate

For 2 portions:

2 level tablespoons cocoa	1 level teaspoon instant coffee
1 level dessertspoon custard powder	1 pint milk
2 level tablespoons castor sugar	

1. Place cocoa, custard powder, sugar and coffee in a saucepan. Stir in milk, a little at a time, using a wooden spoon.

2. Bring to boil, stirring, then simmer for 2 minutes.

3. Whisk chocolate in saucepan until frothy. Pour into mugs and serve.

The Cooking of Germany, Austria and Hungary

The cooking of these countries is similar in many ways: The Germans like filling and substantial meals. They are fond of the sweet and sour combination with meats, as in marinaded roast meat served with fruit. Soups served with dumplings or pasta are also popular. Pork and pork products are eaten, too: for example, smoked pork, ham and sausages. There is a variety of delicious breads. The Viennese empire included people of several nationalities who have influenced Austrian food. Veal is very common in Austria, and milk, cream, butter and cheese are plentiful.

Hungarian food is both satisfying and delicious. Typical ingredients are: paprika, onions, green peppers, tomatoes, sour cream, pasta. Piquant-flavoured veal, pork and beef stews are liked.

Germany

Kartoffelsuppe mit Kartoffelklössen (Potato Soup with Potato Dumplings)

1

3

2

4

Potato soup is a favourite starter for a meal—it's the first soup a German girl learns to make. It is almost a meal in itself, and can also be served as an enjoyable supper dish.

ingredients

For 4 portions:
1½lb potatoes
2 medium-sized carrots
1 leek
1 stick of celery
2 medium-sized onions
7oz streaky bacon
2 slices white bread from a large loaf
1 beef stock cube

1 pint boiling water
½oz margarine
Salt and pepper
¼ level teaspoon marjoram
4oz salami in one piece
1 standard egg
Nutmeg
Cornflour
Parsley
3 tablespoons oil or fat for frying

method

1. Peel potatoes and carrots and boil 1lb of the potatoes until tender. Cut remaining potatoes into ½in dice. Trim off roots, some of the green tops and any tough outside leaves from leek. Cut leek halfway through lengthwise; open out and wash thoroughly to remove any soil, then cut into rings. Wash and slice celery; cut carrots into rings. Peel and slice onions. Remove rind and bone from bacon, reserving rind, and cut bacon into small pieces. Cut off crusts from bread,

then cut bread into ½in cubes. Dissolve stock cube in boiling water.

2. Melt margarine in a saucepan; fry bacon and bacon rind for 1 minute; add carrots, leek, celery and onions and cook over a low heat for a further 5 minutes, stirring occasionally. Add stock, 1 pint water, ½ level teaspoon salt, ¼ level teaspoon pepper and marjoram. Bring to boil, cover tightly; simmer for 10 minutes. Remove bacon rind; add diced potatoes. Cover and continue cooking for a further 10 minutes. Remove skin from salami; cut into ¼in dice and add to saucepan. Simmer for a further 5 minutes.

3. Sieve cooked potatoes into a bowl. Beat egg and add, together with a little salt, pepper, grated nutmeg and 2oz cornflour; mix well. Turn out on to a board, lightly dredged with cornflour. Form into a roll and divide into 8 even-sized pieces; shape into dumplings. Fill a large saucepan two-thirds full with water, add some salt and put to heat. Blend 1 rounded teaspoon cornflour with a little cold water, add to saucepan and bring to boil, stirring; add dumplings. Remove saucepan from heat and leave for 10 minutes. Chop parsley.

4. Fry bread cubes in oil or a little fat in a small frying pan, until golden brown and crisp. Drain on crumpled kitchen paper and mix with chopped parsley. Taste soup and add more salt and pepper, if necessary. Remove excess fat with a paper tissue, if necessary. Carefully lift potato dumplings out of liquor and on to a serving plate. Place the croûtons on a serving plate and serve soup separately in a large tureen.

Linsensuppe

(Lentil Soup)

This is a typical German soup. Serve it piping hot with crusty bread for a substantial first course. Add more sliced frankfurters for a nourishing snack meal.

For 4 to 6 portions:

1 onion	1oz margarine
2 carrots	1 tablespoon cider
1 parsnip	vinegar (optional)
1 small turnip	2 level teaspoons salt
2 sticks of celery	Black pepper
3 rashers streaky bacon	4 frankfurters
4oz lentils	

1. Peel and thinly slice onion, carrots and parsnip. Peel turnip; cut into ¼in dice. Wash and slice celery.

2. Remove rind and bone from bacon; cut bacon into strips. Place lentils in a colander and wash under cold running water.

3. Melt margarine in a large saucepan. Add bacon and cook for 1 minute. Add vegetables and lentils and cook for about 5 minutes, stirring occasionally.

4. Add 2 pints water, vinegar, if used, salt and a shake of pepper. Bring to boil; cover and simmer for about 1 hour, until vegetables are tender.

5. Cut frankfurters into ¼in slices and add to soup. Cook for a further 5 to 10 minutes. Pour into a soup tureen and serve piping hot.

Kolbaszos Rantotta

(Scrambled Eggs with Sausage)

The Hungarian Gyulai sausage used in this recipe can be bought in delicatessens, but boiling sausage may be substituted. Serve this dish for breakfast, as they do in Hungary, or for a light snack.

For 4 portions:

2oz unsmoked, streaky bacon	6 standard eggs
¼lb Gyulai sausage	6 tablespoons milk
1 green pepper	¼ level teaspoon salt
1½oz margarine	Pepper

1. Remove rind and bone from bacon; cut bacon into small pieces. Slice sausage; cut slices into quarters. Cut green pepper in half lengthwise; discard seeds, core and white pith. Cut pepper into large dice.

2. Fry bacon, sausage and green pepper in margarine in a saucepan for about 5 minutes.

3. Place eggs, milk, salt and a shake of pepper in a bowl and beat well together. Add to saucepan. Stir over a low heat, until thick and lightly scrambled. Serve immediately with buttered toast or crusty bread.

Rakott Burgonya

(Potato and Egg Dish)

In Hungary, this is a breakfast dish, but it also makes an excellent supper or light luncheon dish.

For 6 portions:

1½lb potatoes	4oz cooked, sliced ham
6 standard eggs	Salt and pepper
1 medium-sized cauliflower	½oz fresh white
1 (5 (fluid oz) carton soured	breadcrumbs
cream	2oz butter, melted
3 tablespoons milk	

1. Prepare a moderate oven (350 deg F, Gas Mark 4). Butter a deep, 3-pint, ovenproof casserole.

2. Peel potatoes, cut into slices and cook in boiling, salted water until tender; drain.

3. Hard boil eggs for 10 minutes; crack and leave to cool in cold water. Shell and dry on kitchen paper; slice.

4. Discard outer leaves from cauliflower; cut cauliflower into sprigs. Cook in boiling, salted water for 12 minutes, or until tender; drain well. Place soured cream and milk in a basin and mix together with a fork.

5. Arrange half the potatoes in the casserole, cover with the ham, pour over one-third of cream and milk and sprinkle with salt and pepper. Arrange hard-boiled eggs over, sprinkle with salt and pepper and pour over another one-third cream and milk. Arrange cauliflower on top, pour over remaining cream and milk. Top with potatoes and sprinkle with breadcrumbs and some salt; trickle over melted butter.

6. Place just above centre of oven and cook for 35 minutes, until lightly browned.

Rollmops

These are boned herrings, rolled up with a filling of chopped onions, gherkins and peppercorns, and preserved in spiced vinegar. They are popular in Germany and are sold in delicatessens in this country. Follow our recipe, if you prefer to make your own.

To 8 herrings allow:

2oz cooking salt	½ pint boiling water

SPICED VINEGAR:

½ pint vinegar	1 large onion
3 level tablespoons pickling	12 cocktail gherkins
spice (only 2 chillis)	24 peppercorns
1 rounded teaspoon sugar	1 bay leaf

1. Dissolve salt in ½ pint boiling water and leave until cold.

2. Cut off the heads of herrings, using a sharp knife. Scrape the skin with a round-ended knife, from tail to head, to remove scales. Wash under running water.

3. Cut along underside of each fish, from head to tail; remove roe. Gently scrape away any gut and blood vessels.

4. Open fish and place, skin uppermost, on a board. Press firmly all the way along centre back of the fish to loosen backbone.

5. Turn fish over and ease away backbone from flesh, starting at head end. Place herrings in a casserole and pour over salted water. Cover and place in a refrigerator for 2 hours.

6. Make spiced vinegar: Place vinegar, ¼ pint water, pickling spice and sugar in a saucepan; bring to boil. Remove from heat and leave until cold. Strain, discarding pickling spice.

7. Pour water off herrings and rinse well in cold water. Peel and chop onion. Slice gherkins. Lay herrings out flat, skin side down, and place some onion, gherkin and 3 peppercorns on each. Roll up, from head to tail, and tie with cotton. Place in jars or a casserole, add bay leaf and cover completely with spiced vinegar. Keep in a refrigerator or cold place for at least 5 days before eating. Rollmops will keep for 3 to 4 weeks.

Rollmop Salad

Use home-made or bought rollmops for this delicious salad.

For 4 portions:

1lb potatoes	*¼lb carrots*

FRENCH DRESSING:

3 tablespoons oil	*Pepper*
2 tablespoons vinegar	*Pinch of dry mustard*
¼ level teaspoon salt	*Pinch of sugar*

4 spring onions	*6 cocktail gherkins*
1 lettuce	*4 rollmops*
1 small cooked beetroot	*1 small eating apple*

1. Wash and peel potatoes and carrots; cut potatoes into ½ in dice and slice carrots. Cook in boiling, salted water for about 5 to 10 minutes, until just tender. Drain and rinse in cold water.

2. To make French dressing: Place all dressing ingredients in a bowl and beat with a fork. Add potatoes and carrots. Stir carefully, until coated with dressing; leave until cold.

3. Wash and slice spring onions. Wash, dry and shred lettuce. Peel and cut beetroot into ¼ in dice. Slice gherkins. Remove onion from rollmops; cut off tails. Cut rollmops in halves lengthwise, then into 1in pieces.

4. Wash, quarter and core apple; cut into thin slices, leaving skin on. Add spring onions, beetroot, gherkins, rollmops and apple to bowl. Stir mixture carefully to mix. Arrange shredded lettuce on a serving dish and pile salad on top.

Jungfernbraten

(Virgin's Roast)

The literal translation of this name is certainly strange and its derivation is not known. However, it is an unusual and delicious way of serving belly of pork.

For 4 or 5 portions:

2lb lean end belly of pork	*1 level tablespoon plain*
1 medium-sized onion	*flour*
2 carrots	*1 rounded teaspoon capers*
1 small parsnip	*1 (5 fluid oz) carton soured*
1 level teaspoon paprika	*cream*
Salt	*1 rounded teaspoon chopped*
¼ level teaspoon pepper	*parsley*
1oz lard	

1. Ask butcher to bone meat and remove the skin. Place bones in a saucepan, cover with water and simmer for 1 hour; strain off stock and reserve.

2. Prepare a moderate oven (350 deg F, Gas Mark 4).

3. Peel onion and cut into quarters. Peel and slice carrots and parsnip. Roll up meat and tie with string. Place paprika, 1 rounded teaspoon salt and pepper in a basin; mix together and rub over meat. Heat lard in a frying pan and fry vegetables for 5 minutes until lightly browned. Place vegetables in a deep, 4-pint casserole or meat tin; stir in some salt, flour and ¼ pint of the stock.

4. Place meat on vegetables in casserole. Cover and cook just above centre of oven for 1 hour. Remove lid and continue cooking for a further 30 minutes. Add a little extra stock, if necessary. Chop capers.

5. Place meat on a warmed serving dish; remove string. Arrange vegetables around meat and keep hot. Leave stock in casserole. Using either a spoon or kitchen paper, skim off fat from stock in casserole. Stir in soured cream, capers and parsley. Taste and add more salt and pepper, if necessary. Return to oven for a few minutes to heat through. Pour a little sauce over pork and serve remainder separately.

Hungary

Goulash

1

3

2

4

PAPRIKA: This spice is made from sweet capsicum peppers, which grow particularly well in Hungary. It has a mild, pungent flavour and a delicious aroma. It must not be confused with Cayenne pepper or chilli powder, both of which look similar, but are only used in small quantities, as they are very hot. Paprika is used as a garnish or in teaspoonsful or tablespoonsful in soups and meat dishes to add colour and flavour. In cooking, it is usually added to the other ingredients and not fried on its own in hot fat like other pungent spices.

ingredients

For 4 portions:
1 large onion
¾ lb tomatoes
3 rounded teaspoons plain flour
1 rounded teaspoon salt
¼ level teaspoon pepper
1¼ lb pie pork
1 medium-sized green pepper (optional)
1oz lard
1 level tablespoon paprika
2 rounded teaspoons tomato purée

½ pint stock or ½ pint water and 1 golden meat extract cube
1 rounded teaspoon castor sugar
1 bay leaf
A little grated nutmeg

DUMPLINGS:
4oz self-raising flour
½ level teaspoon salt
1½ oz shredded suet
Cold water to mix

A little parsley
1 (5 fluid oz) carton soured cream

method

1. Prepare a moderate oven (350 deg F, Gas Mark 4). Peel and slice onion. Place tomatoes in a bowl and cover with boiling water. Leave for about 1 minute, drain, then peel and slice. Mix together flour, salt and pepper in a bowl. Trim off any excess fat from pork and cut meat into 1in dice; coat in seasoned flour. Cut green pepper in half lengthwise, if used; discard seeds, core and white pith. Slice into strips.

2. Heat lard in a large saucepan and fry onion for 3 to 4 minutes. Add paprika and meat, and fry lightly. Stir in tomato purée, tomatoes, green pepper, stock (or water and meat extract cube), sugar, bay leaf and nutmeg. Bring to boil, stirring. Pour into a 3-pint casserole, cover, and cook in the centre of oven for 1 hour.

3. Place flour, salt and suet in a bowl and mix to a soft, but not sticky, dough with water. Turn out on to a floured board and knead lightly. Divide into 12 even-sized pieces; form into dumplings. Remove bay leaf from goulash, then taste and add more salt and pepper, if necessary. Arrange dumplings around edge of casserole. Cover and return to oven for a further 20 minutes or until dumplings are well risen and cooked through. Chop parsley.

4. Just before serving, carefully stir in soured cream and sprinkle with chopped parsley. Serve with green salad.

Note: Stewing steak or pie veal may be used instead of pork.

Rheinischer Sauerbraten

(Rhine-style Braised Beef)
(pictured on back cover)

Many German savoury dishes are cooked with sweet and sour flavourings, and are served with fruits. This typical braised meat dish is very popular in Germany. You'll find it makes a pleasant change from traditional-style braised beef.

For 4 to 6 portions:
MARINADE:

3 medium-sized onions	12 peppercorns
2 medium-sized carrots	1 bay leaf
¼ pint wine vinegar	3 cloves
1 level teaspoon salt	
1 rounded teaspoon	
granulated sugar	

BRAISED BEEF:

2lb joint silverside	1 level teaspoon tomato
1 stick of celery	purée
Salt	4oz raisins
2oz streaky bacon	½oz cornflour
½oz lard	Gravy browning (optional)
1 level tablespoon	
redcurrant jelly	

1. Peel and slice onions and carrots. Place, with 1 pint water, vinegar, salt, sugar, peppercorns, bay leaf and cloves in a saucepan. Bring to boil and boil quickly for 1 minute; remove from heat. Wash meat in cold water; place in a bowl. Pour marinade over; cover with foil and cool quickly. Place in a refrigerator or cold place for 3 days, turning meat occasionally.

2. Prepare a moderate oven (375 deg F, Gas Mark 5). Wash and slice celery. Drain meat well and dry on kitchen paper; sprinkle all over with salt. Strain marinade and reserve. Remove rind and bone from bacon; cut bacon into small pieces. Heat lard in a flameproof casserole or roasting tin; add bacon and fry for 1 minute. Add beef and fry quickly on all sides, until the fat is browned; remove beef.

3. Add the marinade vegetables and celery to casserole; cook for 5 minutes, stirring occasionally. Stir in redcurrant jelly, tomato purée and ¾ pint marinade; bring to boil, stirring. Place beef in centre, baste with sauce and place in centre of oven.

4. Cook for 1½ hours, basting occasionally (add more marinade, if required, during cooking). Lift beef out on to a warmed serving dish; remove string and keep warm. Strain gravy into a measuring jug and make up to ¾ pint with marinade. Pour into a saucepan, add raisins, bring to boil and simmer for 5 minutes. Blend cornflour to a smooth paste with a little cold water. Remove gravy from heat and stir in blended cornflour; bring to boil, stirring, and simmer for 3 minutes. (Colour with a little gravy browning, if desired.) Pour a little over meat, and remainder into a warmed sauceboat. Serve with Vanilla Apples (see following recipe), green beans and mashed potatoes.

Vanille Apfelspalten

(Vanilla Apples)

4 small cooking apples	6oz granulated sugar
Boiling water	½ teaspoon vanilla essence
Pared rind of 1 lemon	

1. Peel, quarter, core and slice apples; place in a saucepan, cover with boiling water and simmer for 2 to 3 minutes, until just tender.

2. Place lemon rind, ½ pint water, sugar and vanilla essence together in a saucepan. Bring to boil, stirring; remove from heat.

3. Strain apples and add to hot syrup; leave until cold. Remove lemon rind, strain and serve apples with Rheinischer Sauerbraten or Schweinefleisch Mit Apfeln.

Schweinskoteletten mit Apfeln

(Pork Chops with Apples)

For 4 portions:

4 pork chops	1 rounded teaspoon salt
1 small onion	¼ level teaspoon pepper
1 standard egg	2oz fresh white breadcrumbs
1 level tablespoon chopped	4oz lard
parsley	Vanilla Apples (see recipe
1 level teaspoon dried sage	above)

1. Trim pork chops. Peel and chop onion. Place egg in a large, shallow dish or casserole. Beat egg and add onion, parsley, sage, salt and pepper; mix well. Place chops in dish; turn over to coat in beaten egg mixture. Cover and leave for 1 hour, turning chops over occasionally.

2. Remove chops and brush off any excess onion, parsley or sage; coat in breadcrumbs.

3. Heat lard in a frying pan and fry chops for 15 to 20 minutes, turning once, until golden brown on both sides; drain on kitchen paper. Serve with Vanilla Apples.

Chicken Paprika

For 4 portions:

2 medium-sized onions	3 level teaspoons tomato
1oz plain flour	purée
1 level teaspoon salt	1 level teaspoon castor
Pepper	sugar
1 level teaspoon paprika	1 (5 fluid oz) carton soured
4 chicken joints	cream
1oz margarine	Chopped parsley

1. Peel and chop onions. Mix flour, salt, a shake of pepper and paprika together. Trim chicken joints and coat in seasoned flour.

2. Melt margarine in a large frying pan. Fry onion for 2 minutes, add chicken joints and fry until lightly browned.

3. Stir any remaining flour into pan. Add tomato purée, ½ pint water and sugar. Cover and simmer for 30 minutes or until chicken is cooked.

4. Stir soured cream into frying pan; pour on to a warmed serving dish and sprinkle with chopped parsley. Serve immediately with noodles or rice and crisp green salad.

Hunter's Beef Stew

Green pepper and vinegar add a piquant flavour to this delicious Austrian stew. It is thickened by the addition of rice towards the end of the cooking time.

For 4 portions:

4 rashers streaky bacon	*1½ pints beef stock or 1*
2 small onions	*beef stock cube dissolved*
2 medium-sized carrots	*in 1½ pints boiling water*
1 clove of garlic	*3 tablespoons malt vinegar*
1 rounded teaspoon salt	*¼ level teaspoon pepper*
1¼lb chuck steak	*1 green pepper*
½oz lard	*4oz long-grain rice*

1. Remove rind and bone from bacon; cut bacon into strips. Peel and chop onions. Peel and slice carrots. Peel clove of garlic and place on a saucer with salt. Using a round-ended knife, rub salt against garlic to crush clove. Trim off any excess fat from steak and cut meat into 1in dice.

2. Heat lard in a large saucepan; fry bacon for 5 minutes. Remove from saucepan and place on a plate, reserving fat in saucepan. Add onions, carrots and meat to saucepan; fry for about 5 minutes.

3. Stir in stock, vinegar, garlic, bacon and pepper. Bring to boil, cover and simmer for 1¼ to 1½ hours.

4. Cut green pepper in half lengthwise; discard seeds, core and white pith. Slice pepper into strips. Add to stew with rice and cook for a further 25 to 30 minutes, adding more stock or water, if necessary, until rice is tender and meat cooked. Serve with a green vegetable.

Wiener Schnitzel

(Fried Escalopes of Veal)

This is, perhaps, the most famous Austrian recipe and is often served in different ways. However, the traditional Austrian way is very simple, as shown in the following recipe.

For 4 portions:

4 veal escalopes, each	*1 standard egg*
weighing 4oz to 5oz	*3oz fresh white breadcrumbs*
1½oz plain flour	*4oz lard*
1 rounded teaspoon salt	*Lemon wedges*
¼ level teaspoon pepper	*Parsley*

1. Trim veal. Wet a sheet of greaseproof paper. Place on a board, wet side up, arrange escalopes over and cover with another sheet of wetted greaseproof paper, wet side down. Beat well with the side of a rolling pin, to flatten. (Your butcher may do this for you.) Snip edges of veal. Place flour, salt and pepper on a plate; mix together. Place egg and 1 tablespoon cold water on another plate; beat together with a fork. Place breadcrumbs on another plate.

2. Coat escalopes in seasoned flour and shake off any excess; coat in beaten egg and allow any excess to drain off. Finally, coat in breadcrumbs, shaking off excess.

3. Heat 2oz lard in a large frying pan; fry 2 escallops for 5 minutes, turning once, until crisp and golden brown on both sides and cooked through. Drain on kitchen paper and keep hot, while frying remaining 2 escalopes in remaining lard. Serve immediately with lemon wedges and garnish with sprigs of parsley.

Saurer Kohl mit Schweinsrippchen

(Sour Cabbage with Pork)

For 4 portions:

1lb firm white cabbage	*Pinch of ground black*
1 large cooking apple	*pepper*
1 large onion	*1 level tablespoon brown*
1oz dripping	*sugar*
1 tablespoon vinegar	*4 pork chops*
1 level teaspoon salt	

1. Wash and shred cabbage, peel and core apple and cut into chunks; peel and slice onion.

2. Melt dripping in a saucepan and fry the onion for 2 to 3 minutes. Add cabbage, apple, 2 tablespoons water, vinegar, salt, pepper and sugar. Cover with a tight-fitting lid and cook slowly for 25 to 30 minutes until cabbage is tender and has turned pinky-brown in colour.

3. Meanwhile, prepare a moderate grill and cook chops until tender, about 20 minutes.

4. To serve: Place cabbage on a warmed serving dish and arrange chops on top.

Mandel Splitter

(Almond Biscuits)

Makes about 20:

1oz blanched almonds	*2oz ground almonds*
2 egg whites	*2oz plain chocolate*
2oz icing sugar	

1. Prepare a very cool oven (225 deg F, Gas Mark ¼). Finely chop blanched almonds. Brush 2 baking sheets with oil or melted fat and line with greaseproof paper; grease paper.

2. Place egg whites in a clean, grease-free bowl and whisk until stiff, but not dry. Whisk in half the sugar. Fold in remaining sugar and ground almonds.

3. Spread mixture out to rounds, about 2½in in diameter, on baking sheets; sprinkle with chopped almonds.

4. Bake in centre of oven for 25 to 30 minutes. Biscuits should be firm, but not crisp or browned. Remove from paper and place on a rolling pin for a few minutes to curve the biscuits.

5. Break up chocolate and place in a dry basin over a saucepan of hot, but not boiling, water; stir occasionally until melted. Remove basin from saucepan and spread the underside of each biscuit with chocolate; leave to harden.

Germany

Schwarzwälder Kirschtorte （Black Forest Cherry Cake）

1

3

2

4

CHERRIES: In Germany, tart, delicious bottled Morello cherries are used for this cake, and the syrup is thickened with cornflour. Although sometimes available in cans, these cherries are not easy to find in this country. A can of cherry pie filling is the nearest substitute.

KIRSCH: This liqueur is made from cherries, the kernels giving added flavour. It is not as sweet as cherry brandy, and is used for flavouring fruit salads and confectionery, too. It's also known as Kirschwasser.

ingredients

For 8 to 10 portions:
SPONGE:
3 large eggs
6oz castor sugar
6oz plain flour
2 level tablespoons cocoa
2 level teaspoons baking powder
4 tablespoons hot water

FILLING AND
DECORATION:
1 (5 fluid oz) carton double cream
1 small (2⅞ fluid oz) carton double cream
1 (5 fluid oz) carton single cream
1 tablespoon cold milk
2 tablespoons kirsch liqueur (optional)
1 (14¼oz) can cherry pie filling
1oz plain chocolate

method

1. Prepare a moderate oven (375 deg F, Gas Mark 5). Brush a deep, round 8½in cake tin with melted fat and line base with greaseproof paper; grease paper. Bring a saucepan of water to boil and remove from heat. Place eggs and sugar in a bowl and whisk over saucepan until mixture thickens, and leaves a trail when lifted. Remove bowl from saucepan and continue whisking until mixture is cool. Sift flour, cocoa and baking powder together; carefully fold into egg mixture, cutting through mixture with a metal spoon. Fold in hot water. Pour into prepared tin and bake in centre of oven for about 35 to 40 minutes. Test by pressing with the fingers. If cooked, cake should spring back, have stopped bubbling and have begun to shrink from side of tin. Turn out, remove paper and leave to cool on a wire rack.

2. Place double and single creams and milk in a basin and whisk until just stiff. When cool, cut cake into 3 horizontally: Using a sharp knife, make 2 horizontal cuts to divide cake into 3, from highest point (not from top edge). Cut evenly around edge, following line of both cuts. With a long knife, cut top section through to centre, turning cake, until cut is right through layer; remove top layer and cut remaining piece similarly.

3. Sprinkle bottom layer of sponge with some kirsch, if used. Place one-third of cream in a piping bag fitted with a large star tube and pipe a band of cream around edge. Reserve 7 cherries from pie filling for decoration. Remove 4 tablespoons of sauce from can (this may be served with ice cream, yoghourt or other foods) and spread remainder in centre of sponge up to band of cream.

4. Place centre layer of sponge on top and sprinkle with a little kirsch; spread with about one-third of remaining cream. Sprinkle underside of top layer of sponge with remaining kirsch. Invert on to cream layer. Spread remaining cream on top and around side of cake. Coarsely grate chocolate and sprinkle over top and around side of cake. Pipe 14 whirls of cream around top edge of cake and top each alternate whirl with a cherry. Keep the cake in a cool place until it is ready to serve.

Haselnusstorte

(Hazelnut Cake)

Hazelnuts are very popular in Germany, Austria and Hungary, and are frequently used in their cake and biscuit recipes. The fresh breadcrumbs, used in place of flour, and whisked egg whites give this cake a very light texture.

For 8 to 12 portions:

6oz hazelnuts
5 standard eggs
Castor sugar
2oz fresh white breadcrumbs
1 (5 fluid oz) carton
double cream

1 (5 fluid oz) carton
single cream
½ teaspoon vanilla essence

1. Prepare a moderate oven (375 deg F, Gas Mark 5). Brush a deep, round 8in cake tin with melted fat. Line bottom and side with greaseproof paper; grease paper.

2. Place hazelnuts in a roasting tin; place in top of oven and leave for about 10 to 15 minutes until golden brown. Rub off skins, reserve 7 nuts for decoration, then either grate remainder or place in an electric grinder or liquidiser goblet and run machine for 2 to 3 seconds, until roughly ground.

3. Separate eggs, placing yolks in a bowl and whites in a separate clean, grease-free bowl. Add 5oz sugar to egg yolks and whisk together until mixture is thick and leaves a trail when whisk is lifted.

4. Whisk egg whites until stiff, but not dry. Lightly fold egg whites, 4oz of the ground hazelnuts and breadcrumbs into whisked egg yolks and sugar with a metal spoon. Pour into cake tin and bake in centre of oven for 40 to 50 minutes. Test by pressing with the fingers. If cooked, cake should spring back and have begun to shrink from side of tin. Remove cake from tin and leave to cool on a wire rack; when cool, remove paper. Store cake in a tin overnight, before cutting.

5. Place double and single creams in a bowl with vanilla essence and 1 rounded teaspoon sugar; whisk until just stiff.

6. Cut cake into 3 horizontally: Using a sharp knife, make 2 horizontal cuts to divide cake into 3, from highest point (not from top edge). Cut evenly around edge, following line of both cuts. With a long knife, cut top section through to centre, turning cake, until cut is through layer; remove top layer and cut remaining piece similarly.

7. Spread a quarter of cream over bottom layer of cake. Place centre layer of cake on top and spread another quarter of cream over. Place remaining layer of cake on top.

8. Place a quarter of remaining cream in a piping bag, fitted with a large star tube. Spread some cream around the side of cake.

9. Place remaining ground hazelnuts on a piece of greaseproof paper. Hold top and bottom of cake and roll side in ground hazelnuts. Spread top of cake with remaining cream. Pipe whirls of cream around top edge of cake and place reserved 7 hazelnuts at equal intervals on top. Keep the cake in a cool place until it is ready to serve.

Zwetschgenkuchen vom Blech

(Plum Cake)

This delicious dessert is traditionally made with zwetzen plums, which are firm when cooked. However, it may be made with other types of plums, preferably a small, not too juicy variety.

For 12 portions:
YEAST LIQUID:

1 level teaspoon castor sugar
4 fluid oz hand-hot milk
(110 deg F)

2 level teaspoons
dried yeast

DOUGH:

8oz plain flour
1oz castor sugar
Finely-grated rind of
half a lemon

¼ level teaspoon cinnamon
1 standard egg
½ level teaspoon salt

TOPPING:

1oz fresh white breadcrumbs
1lb plums

4 rounded tablespoons castor
sugar

1. Dissolve 1 level teaspoon sugar in the milk in a small basin; sprinkle on yeast and leave until frothy, about 10 minutes.

2. Place flour, sugar, lemon rind and cinnamon in a bowl; mix together. Beat egg and salt together in a small basin.

3. Add yeast liquid and egg to flour mixture; mix until smooth. Beat thoroughly for 10 minutes, stretching the dough well.

4. Cover bowl with greased polythene or foil. Leave to rise for about 1 hour, or until dough has doubled in size and will spring back when pressed with a floured finger. Grease a baking sheet.

5. Turn out dough on to a lightly floured board and knead to disperse any large air bubbles. Roll out to an oblong, 12in by 8in, and place on baking sheet. Pinch up edges about ½in, so that the oblong measures 11in by 7in. Sprinkle with breadcrumbs.

6. Wash plums; cut in halves and remove stones. Make a small cut in each plum half at each end. Arrange plums on dough, cut sides uppermost. Leave in a warm place for 30 minutes or until dough has doubled in thickness.

7. Prepare a hot oven (425 deg F, Gas Mark 7).

8. Bake in centre of oven for 10 to 15 minutes until dough is golden brown and plums are tender. Remove from oven and sprinkle with sugar. Carefully lift on to a wire rack and leave to cool. When cold, cut into 12 rectangular portions. Serve with whipped cream.

Note: Alternatively, use fresh yeast: Warm measured milk and blend in ½oz yeast (omit 1 level teaspoon sugar) and use at once.

Topfentorte

(Cheesecake)

Typical of one of the varieties of Continental cheesecake, it is firmer and less rich than Kentucky Cheesecake (see recipe on page 88).

For 9 portions:
PASTRY:

6oz plain flour	*1 egg yolk*
½ level teaspoon salt	*Cold water to mix*
3oz margarine	*Beaten egg or milk to*
2 level tablespoons castor	*glaze*
sugar	

FILLING:

1lb curd cheese	*4oz castor sugar*
1 egg white	*1oz sultanas*

1. Prepare a moderate oven (375 deg F, Gas Mark 5). Lightly grease a baking tin, 6½in square and 1½in deep.

2. Place flour and salt in a bowl, add margarine, cut into small pieces; rub in with the fingertips until mixture resembles fine breadcrumbs.

3. Mix in sugar and bind with egg yolk and water to form a firm dough.

4. Roll out two-thirds of pastry and line the bottom and sides of tin. Roll out remaining pastry to an oblong, about 9in by 6in. Cut into strips, ¼in wide and 9in long.

5. Place all ingredients for filling in a bowl and mix well; turn into pastry-lined tin. Arrange pastry strips in a lattice pattern, spaced about ¼in apart, over filling and press down lightly; trim ends. Brush with beaten egg or milk.

6. Cook in centre of oven for 45 to 50 minutes until golden brown. Leave to cool for 30 minutes in tin, then turn out on to a wire rack. To serve, cut into 2in squares.

Linzertorte

For 5 or 6 portions:

5oz butter	*6oz plain flour*
4oz castor sugar	*1 level teaspoon ground*
1 egg yolk	*cinnamon*
½ teaspoon almond essence	*2oz ground almonds*
Grated rind of 1 small	*½lb raspberry jam*
lemon	*Icing sugar*
Juice of half a small lemon	

1. Prepare a cool oven (325 deg F, Gas Mark 3). Place a 7in plain flan ring on a baking sheet; grease baking sheet inside flan ring and inside edge of ring.

2. Cream butter and sugar together until light and fluffy. Beat in egg yolk, almond essence, lemon rind and juice.

3. Add flour, cinnamon and ground almonds; mix well and knead in bowl until smooth. Wrap in foil; leave in a cool place for 1 hour.

4. Place three-quarters of the mixture in flan ring and press over base and up side so that the mixture comes ¼in above top of flan ring. Spread jam over base.

5. Divide remaining mixture in half and roll between the hands into 2 long (17½in) strips. Cut each strip into 1 (6½in) piece and 2 (5½in) pieces. Arrange strips in a lattice pattern across flan. Run a knife around top of flan ring to loosen mixture from side. Press down mixture to form a border, about ½in wide, covering ends of lattice.

6. Bake in centre of oven for 1 hour or until golden brown; remove from oven and leave to cool. Remove flan ring and dredge torte with icing sugar. Serve cold, with whipped cream.

Note: This torte improves in flavour, if kept for 2 to 3 days.

Kaiserschmarren

(Emperor's Broken Pancake)

This recipe is attributed to the Emperor Franz Joseph I. One story about it says that while he was out hunting in the Tyrol, he called at a peasant's home for a meal. The daughter made a pancake and, because she was so nervous cooking for the Emperor, she broke it and burst into tears. Her mother, however, rose to the occasion, broke the pancake into small pieces and served it as their speciality! Whether this story is true or not, the pancake is well worth making.

For 3 or 4 portions:

3oz plain flour	*¼ pint milk*
Castor sugar	*1oz sultanas*
1oz butter	*3 rounded tablespoons jam*
2 standard eggs	*Lard for frying*

1. Place flour and 1oz sugar in a mixing bowl. Make a 'well' in centre. Melt butter in a small saucepan; remove from heat. Separate eggs, placing the whites in a clean, grease-free bowl. Place yolks with milk and melted butter in a bowl and beat together. Gradually stir half of milk mixture into flour and sugar. Mix well, using a wooden spoon, and beat until smooth; add remainder of milk mixture.

2. Whisk egg whites until stiff, but not dry. Fold egg whites and sultanas into mixture.

3. To make jam sauce: Place jam and 3 tablespoons water in a small saucepan. Place over a moderate heat and bring to boil, stirring. Cover, remove from heat and keep hot.

4. Heat a little lard in a large frying pan. Pour off any excess lard into a small bowl, leaving pan lightly greased. Pour all the batter into pan to thickly coat the base. Cook over a moderate heat until underside is golden brown.

5. Hold pan over a tray (in case of accidents). Using a fish slice, quickly flip pancake over. Cook until brown on other side. Using 2 forks, tear the pancake into small pieces. Turn out on to a warmed serving dish, sprinkle with castor sugar and serve with jam sauce.

Austria

Apfelstrudel

1

3

2

4

STRUDEL PASTRY: This is paper thin; it can form a casing for a variety of delicious sweet fillings, the moist fruity ones being the most delicious. Some savoury fillings are used in Austria: cottage or cream cheese, kraut (cabbage) fried with onions and caraway seeds, and minced or chopped ham mixed with thick gravy. For a change, use two fillings for the two halves of dough. Try these fillings:

APPLE AND APRICOT: 8oz dried apricots, 8oz granulated sugar, 1½lb cooking apples, 4oz blanched almonds, 1 level teaspoon mixed spice. Cook apricots and sugar in 1 pint water in a covered saucepan for 35 to 40 minutes. Drain apricots, reserving syrup, and chop. Peel, core and very thinly slice apples. Chop almonds. Place apricots, syrup, apples, almonds and mixed spice together in a bowl and mix well.

CHERRY: 1½lb cherries (Morello, if possible), 2oz blanched almonds, 8oz seedless raisins, 4oz castor sugar, ½ level teaspoon cinnamon. Stone cherries. Chop almonds. Mix all ingredients together.

ingredients

For 8 portions:

STRUDEL PASTRY:
11oz plain flour
½ level teaspoon salt
1 standard egg, beaten
1 tablespoon oil
¼ pint warm water

FILLING:
2lb cooking apples
4oz raisins
6oz castor sugar
½ level teaspoon cinnamon
2oz butter
Icing sugar

method

1. Sift flour and salt together into a bowl. Add beaten egg, oil and water. Mix well, then turn out on to a floured board and knead until smooth. Place dough in a floured polythene bag and leave to rest in a warm (not hot) place for about 1 hour. Prepare a moderately hot oven (400 deg F, Gas Mark 6). Lightly grease a large baking sheet. Peel, core and very thinly slice apples. Place in a bowl and mix in raisins, sugar and cinnamon. Place butter in a small basin and put in oven to melt. Cut pastry in half; roll out 1 half to an oblong, 10in by 8in, on a well-floured board.

2. Gently stretch pastry with the hands, keeping it as even as possible and taking care not to pull any holes in it, until it measures 15in by 12in; cut off thick edges.

3. Brush pastry with melted butter. Stir apples, then spread half the apples over pastry, leaving a 1in border all round. Fold border on short sides over apple, then roll up, Swiss-roll fashion, starting from a long side. Keep roll as tightly rolled as possible. Carefully lift on to a baking sheet, with join underneath, and brush with melted butter. Repeat, using remaining pastry and apples.

4. Bake strudel in centre of oven until golden brown, 30 to 40 minutes. Leave to cool on baking sheet for 10 minutes, then lift off with a palette knife on to a wire rack. When cold, cut each into 4 pieces, cutting diagonally; cut off thick pastry at each end of strudel rolls. Dredge with icing sugar.

Note: Uncooked strudel pastry will keep in a refrigerator for 2 to 3 days in a floured polythene bag. To use, remove from refrigerator, leave in a warm place for 1 hour; proceed as above.

Dobostorte

This recipe is popular in both Austria and Hungary, but in Hungary it is known as Dobos Torta. The number of sponge layers in this cake varies with different recipes, but five layers are usual and easy to handle.

For 12 portions:
SPONGE:

3 standard eggs
3oz castor sugar
3oz plain flour
½ level teaspoon baking powder

1½oz hazelnuts

1 level teaspoon finely-grated lemon rind

CREME AU BEURRE
(Rich Butter Cream):

3oz granulated sugar
2 standard egg yolks

4oz granulated sugar

3 level tablespoons cocoa
8oz unsalted butter

1. Prepare a moderately hot oven (400 deg F, Gas Mark 6). Cut 3 sheets of greaseproof paper to fit 3 baking sheets. Mark 2 (7in) circles on 2 sheets of paper and 1 (7in) circle on 1 sheet. Brush circles with melted fat.

2. Bring a large saucepan of water to the boil; remove from heat. Place eggs and sugar in a bowl over saucepan and whisk until mixture becomes thick and leaves a trail when whisk is lifted. Remove bowl from saucepan and continue whisking until mixture is cool.

3. Sift flour and baking powder together, add lemon rind, then carefully fold into egg mixture with a metal spoon.

4. Place 3 tablespoons of mixture in each circle on grease-proof paper; spread out to even rounds. Cook 1 baking sheet at a time, just above centre of oven, for 8 to 10 minutes. Test by pressing with the fingers. If cooked, cake should spring back and have stopped bubbling. Place cakes and greaseproof paper on a wire rack and allow to cool for 2 or 3 minutes; carefully remove paper. (If you have only 1 or 2 baking sheets, lift the greaseproof paper with uncooked sponge layers on to baking sheet, after removing cooked sponges.) Using a cake tin or flan ring as a guide, trim sponges to 7in rounds.

5. Place hazelnuts, in a roasting tin, in oven until golden brown, about 10 minutes. Rub off skins, reserve 12 nuts for decoration; coarsely chop remainder.

6. To make crème au beurre: Place 9 tablespoons water and 3oz granulated sugar in a small saucepan; stir over a low heat until sugar has dissolved. Increase heat and boil, without stirring, until syrup registers 220 deg F, on a sugar thermometer, or until syrup forms a thread between 2 teaspoons.

7. Whisk egg yolks in a small bowl, add cocoa and gradually whisk in sugar syrup; continue to whisk until cold.

8. Cut butter into small pieces; whisk into egg mixture, one piece at a time, whisking well after each addition.

9. Place 1 sponge layer on a wire rack over a baking sheet. Place 4oz granulated sugar and 4 tablespoons water in a small saucepan; stir over a low heat until sugar has dissolved. Boil rapidly until deep golden brown. Pour on to sponge and, using a palette knife, spread over surface. While caramel is still hot, using a buttered knife, mark into 12 equal-sized wedges.

10. Reserve half of crème au beurre; spread a quarter of remainder over 1 sponge layer. Place a second layer of sponge on top; continue layering, ending with a layer of crème au beurre. Top with caramel layer of sponge.

11. Spread three-quarters of the reserved crème au beurre around side of cake.

12. Place chopped hazelnuts on a piece of greaseproof paper. Press on to side of cake with a palette knife.

13. Place remaining crème au beurre in a greaseproof paper piping bag; fold down top and snip off end to measure ¼in. Pipe large 'beads' around top edge of cake. Place whole hazelnuts at intervals on beads around edge. Leave cake overnight in a cool place (but not a refrigerator) before serving it.

Berliner Ringe
(Berlin Rings)

Makes 18:

2 standard eggs
4oz margarine
5oz castor sugar
Finely-grated rind of half a small orange

8oz plain flour
Glacé cherries
Angelica

1. Separate 1 egg, placing white in a clean, grease-free bowl and yolk in a basin. Lightly beat white; add half to yolk. Add remaining whole egg and beat together.

2. Cream margarine and 4oz sugar together until light and fluffy. Add eggs gradually, beating well after each addition.

3. Add orange rind and mix in flour. Wrap dough in greaseproof paper and place in a cool place or refrigerator for half an hour.

4. Prepare a moderate oven (350 deg F, Gas Mark 4).

5. Divide dough into 18 equal-sized pieces. With lightly floured hands, form each piece of dough into a roll, about 6in long. Place on baking sheets in rings with ends crossed.

6. Whisk reserved egg white until stiff, but not dry. Whisk in ½oz sugar, then fold in ½oz, cutting through mixture with a metal spoon.

7. Brush meringue on rings. Place a small piece of glacé cherry, with a small angelica 'leaf' on each side, on each ring, where ends cross.

8. Cook just above centre of oven for about 25 minutes or until light golden brown. Leave to cool on a wire rack.

The Cooking of Scandinavia

The most international part of Scandinavian cookery is the Koldt Bord or Smorgasbord, as it is called in Sweden. Cold dishes of herrings, seafood, poultry, meat, pâté, cheese and vegetable salads are displayed buffet-style for guests to help themselves. Norwegian fishermen catch the fish used in the Koldt Bord, which is even served at breakfast time in some hotels.

In Denmark, open sandwiches, known as Smørrebrød (or Danwiches in this country), are served as a first course in homes and restaurants. Simple forms of open sandwiches are carried to work and school in special lunch boxes by the Danes. Dairy foods and pork products are carefully produced in Denmark, and are exported all over the world. The Danes use these foods extensively in their cookery and create some beautifully garnished savoury dishes, as well as the delicious cakes and pastries, for which they are famous.

Scandinavia

Smørrebrød (Danish Open Sandwiches)

Smørrebrød (pronounced smerbrerd) are eaten as a first course or for lunch in Denmark. They would also be ideal for a buffet party or picnic. Serve them with a knife and fork. Smørrebrød are easy to make. They consist of three layers: buttered bread of a firm variety, a savoury topping and an artistically arranged garnish to give height to the sandwich.

ingredients

BASES:
White, brown or French bread or Danish rye bread

TOPPINGS:
Slices of canned chopped ham with pork
Salami
Pâté de foie
Meat
Ham
Liver sausage
Luncheon meat
Chicken
Shrimps
Sardines
Pickled herrings
Tuna

Danish Blue cheese
Danish cheese slices
GARNISHES:
Onion rings
Parsley
Lettuce
Cress
Cucumber twists
Radishes
Watercress
Slices, twists, wedges or quarters of tomato
Gherkin fans
Beetroot
Lemon or orange twists
Stuffed olives
Grapes
Prunes
Scrambled egg
Hard-boiled egg slices
Cream cheese or mayonnaise

method

1. Thickly spread slices of brown bread with butter and top with large, square thin slices of chopped ham with pork, carefully folded to give height. Garnish with raw onion rings and a sprig of parsley.

2. Thickly butter slices of white bread and top with slices of salami and scrambled egg and salami cones. To make cones: Cut 2 slices of salami thinly and remove skin; cut each slice through to the centre; fold around to make a cone and press firmly. Place a little washed cress in the centre of each; arrange on the scrambled egg.

3. Spread slices of Danish rye bread thickly with butter and pâté de foie. Arrange slices of hard-boiled egg on top. Garnish with a tomato twist, lettuce and gherkin fans. To make gherkin fans: Cut through each gherkin from the end to within ¼ in of the stalk end about 4 times. Spread out to make a fan shape and place on hard-boiled eggs.

4. Thickly butter slices of French bread and arrange shrimps on top. Cut thin slices of lemon through to the centre; twist and place on shrimps. Cut and twist 2 cucumber slices in the same way and place on both sides of lemon twist. Garnish with 2 small sprigs of parsley.

Regattakotlett

(Yachtsmen's Pork Chops)

For 4 portions:

4 pork chops
1 level teaspoon paprika
Salt and pepper
1 large onion
1lb tomatoes

1oz lard
¼ level teaspoon dried thyme
Half a bay leaf
Chopped parsley

1. Trim chops. Place paprika, 1 rounded teaspoon salt and a shake of pepper on a plate and mix together; rub over chops. Peel and roughly chop onion. Place tomatoes in a bowl and cover with boiling water. Leave for 1 minute, drain, then peel and cut into small pieces.

2. Heat lard in a frying pan and fry chops for 15 to 20 minutes, turning once. Remove from pan and keep hot.

3. Add onion to pan and fry for 8 to 10 minutes, stirring occasionally, until tender. Add tomatoes, thyme, bay leaf and some salt and pepper. Cook for 2 to 3 minutes.

4. Return chops to pan and cook for a further 2 to 3 minutes. Remove bay leaf. Arrange on a warmed serving dish, sprinkle with parsley and serve with mashed or boiled potatoes.

Frikadeller

(Meat Patties)

There are many versions of these mild-flavoured meat patties in Denmark; each housewife has her own, often closely guarded, recipe. Pork alone is used, or a mixture of pork with veal or beef. Some housewives use soda water in place of milk. Frikadeller are traditionally served with boiled potatoes and pickled beetroot, cucumber or red cabbage.

For 4 portions:

1 small onion
½lb pie pork
½lb lean stewing beef
1 standard egg
1½ level teaspoons salt

Pepper
½ pint milk
4oz plain flour
Fat for frying

1. Peel and quarter onion. Cut meat into strips, discarding fat. Mince meat and onion together.

2. Beat egg, salt and a shake of pepper together; stir in milk.

3. Place flour in a bowl, gradually blend in milk mixture; stir in minced meat and mix well. Leave in a cool place for about 30 minutes.

4. Fry rounded tablespoonsful of mixture in ¼in of hot fat in a frying pan, over a moderate heat, for about 8 minutes on each side, until deep golden brown. Drain on kitchen paper and keep hot while cooking remaining mixture. Serve hot, with boiled or mashed potatoes and a green vegetable.

Sweet and Sour Red Cabbage

For 6 portions:

1 medium-sized red cabbage (weighing about 3lb)
2 large cooking apples
1oz butter
6 tablespoons wine vinegar

2oz granulated sugar
Salt
Black pepper
2 rounded tablespoons redcurrant jelly

1. Wash and shred cabbage. Peel and grate apples.

2. Place cabbage and apples in a saucepan with butter. Cover and cook over a low heat, stirring occasionally, until butter is melted. Add vinegar, 2 tablespoons water and the sugar; cover and simmer for 1 hour.

3. Season with some salt and black pepper; add redcurrant jelly and cook for a further 15 minutes. Serve hot with Roast Goose and Sugar-browned Potatoes (see recipe on page 59) or with roast pork.

Note: This may be made several days before it is required and reheated; it improves with keeping for a few days and may also be served cold.

Ris à l'Amande with Morello Cherry Sauce

After the main course of Roast Goose, the Danes serve Ris à l'Amande for a sweet, as Christmas Eve lunch. This creamy, light pudding would make a delicious alternative for those who find our traditional Christmas pudding too rich. The Danes leave one almond whole in the pudding; the person who finds it in his portion gets a present.

For 4 to 6 portions:

¾ pint milk
¼ vanilla pod or
1 teaspoon vanilla essence
1½oz short-grain pudding rice
1oz shelled almonds

2oz granulated sugar
1 tablespoon sweet sherry
2 level teaspoons gelatine
1 (5 fluid oz) carton double cream

MORELLO CHERRY SAUCE:

1 large (16oz) can Morello cherries

2 level tablespoons cornflour

1. Place milk in a saucepan and bring to boil. Add vanilla and rice. Simmer, uncovered, for about 20 minutes, or until rice is just tender.

2. Place almonds in a small bowl and cover with boiling water. Leave for 1 minute, drain, then remove skins. Keep aside 1 whole almond and chop remainder. Add sugar and sherry to rice; stir well and remove from heat. Remove vanilla pod, if used, and add all the almonds.

3. Measure 1 tablespoon water into a small basin and add gelatine. Place basin in a pan of water over moderate heat and stir until gelatine has dissolved. Add to rice, stir well and pour into a bowl; cover and leave until cold, but not set.

4. Whip cream until thick and lightly fold into rice, a little at a time, using a metal spoon. Pour into a serving dish and leave in a cold place.

5. To make Morello cherry sauce: Strain syrup from can of cherries into a jug, and add 6 tablespoons water. Place cornflour in a saucepan and add syrup gradually, stirring until blended. Bring to boil, stirring, and simmer for 3 minutes. Add cherries and heat through. To serve: Spoon a little hot cherry sauce over rice and serve remainder separately.

Note: A 6oz can of Danish cream, chilled and whipped, can be used instead of fresh double cream, and a can of cherry pie filling instead of Morello cherries and cornflour thickening.

Lucia Buns

In Sweden, these saffron-flavoured buns are made to celebrate the feast of Saint Lucia, on December 13. Small girls, wearing white dresses and with crowns of green leaves and white candles on their heads, carry trays of the buns to their parents' room in the early morning.

Makes 6:

YEAST LIQUID:

Pinch of saffron powder or saffron strands
Boiling water
Milk

1 level teaspoon castor sugar
2 level teaspoons dried yeast

DOUGH:

1oz margarine
8oz strong plain flour

¼ level teaspoon salt
24 seedless raisins

EGG GLAZE:

1 small egg
¼ level teaspoon castor sugar

1. Place saffron in a small basin; add 2 tablespoons boiling water and leave until cool (if using saffron strands, strain). Make up saffron liquid to a scant ¼ pint with milk; add sugar and heat to hand-hot (110 deg F). Sprinkle on yeast and leave until frothy, about 10 minutes. Melt the margarine; leave to cool.

2. Place flour and salt in a bowl; add yeast liquid and margarine. Mix well, adding a little more flour, if necessary, to form a fairly firm dough.

3. Turn out dough on to a floured board and knead and stretch dough, by folding towards you, then pushing away with the palm of the hand. Give dough a quarter turn and

repeat, developing a rocking motion. Knead for about 10 minutes, until dough feels firm and elastic.

4. Place in a lightly-greased polythene bag; leave to rise in a warm place until dough is doubled in size and springs back when pressed with a floured finger, about 1 hour.

5. Turn out dough on to a floured board and knead lightly. Divide dough into 12 equal pieces. Roll each piece into a 9in strip with the hands. Lightly grease a baking sheet. Place 1 strip of dough across another strip, on baking sheet; curl each end in the same direction. Press a raisin in centre of each coil. Repeat with remaining strips.

6. Cover with greased polythene; leave to rise in a warm place for 20 to 30 minutes.

7. Prepare a moderately hot oven (400 deg F, Gas Mark 6). Beat egg, sugar and 1 tablespoon water together.

8. Remove polythene and brush buns with egg glaze. Bake just above centre of oven for 10 to 15 minutes, until golden brown. Leave to cool on a wire rack.

Note: Alternatively, use fresh yeast: Warm saffron liquid and milk, blend in ½oz yeast (omit sugar) and use at once.

Appelkaka
(Apple Pudding)

For 6 portions:

4oz brown bread, without crusts
2lb cooking apples
4oz butter
2oz castor sugar

4 rounded tablespoons redcurrant jelly or raspberry jam
Whipped cream

1. Coarsely grate bread; spread breadcrumbs on a baking tin. Leave in a warm place until crumbs are very dry.

2. Peel, core and slice apples; place in a saucepan with 2oz butter. Cover and cook over a moderate heat, stirring occasionally, until apples are very tender, about 15 minutes. Beat until pulped; leave to cool.

3. Fry breadcrumbs in remaining butter, stirring continuously, until golden brown. Remove from heat; stir in sugar.

4. Spread a quarter of the breadcrumbs in a 2-pint round dish, top with one-third of the apple and spread with a quarter of the jelly or jam. Repeat layering twice more; sprinkle with remaining breadcrumbs. Chill for 3 hours.

5. Just before serving, decorate with swirls of whipped cream and remaining jelly.

Scandinavia

Roast Goose with Sugar-browned potatoes and Red Cabbage

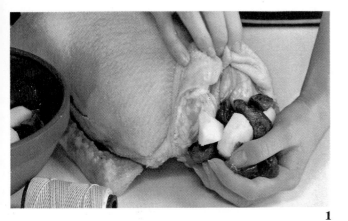

1

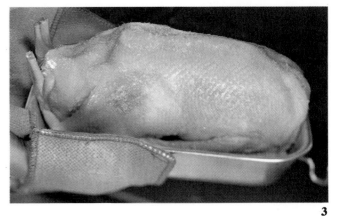

3

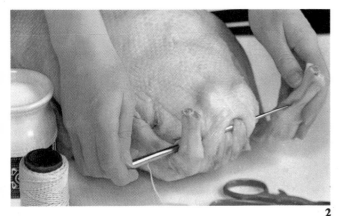

2

4

GOOSE: Choose a young goose, which can be distinguished by its light red or rosy-coloured flesh, pale yellow or white fat and yellow feet. Geese can be bought both fresh and frozen. If frozen, allow to thaw slowly at room temperature for about 24 hours.

TO CARVE: Leave the goose in the oven on its serving dish for 15 minutes before carving, then cut across the leg in thin slices. Slice the breast thinly, starting at the lowest part, beside the leg.

ingredients

For 6 portions:
1 oven-ready goose (about 8lb drawn weight)
Salt and pepper
STUFFING:
½lb prunes
½lb cooking apples
Goose liver, crop and heart

GARNISH:
4 small cooking apples
Redcurrant jelly
Watercress

SUGAR-BROWNED
POTATOES:
1 large (1lb 4½oz) can Danish new potatoes
1oz granulated sugar
1oz butter

method

1. Remove giblets and rinse inside of goose with cold water; dry with kitchen paper. Place giblets in a saucepan, cover with cold water and simmer for 1 hour. Mix together 1 level tablespoon salt and ¼ level teaspoon pepper and rub on inside of goose. To make stuffing: Cut prunes in halves and remove stones. Peel, core and cut apples into small pieces. Remove liver, crop and heart from stock and

cut into small pieces; mix with prunes and apples. Prepare a cool oven (325 deg F, Gas Mark 3). Stuff neck of goose and place any remaining stuffing in body cavity. Weigh goose and calculate cooking time, allowing 15 minutes per lb.

2. Draw the skin backwards over the neck and sew skin flap underneath with a thick needle or trussing needle and fine string. Tuck the tail under skin at the other end of goose, and secure by sewing up with string.

3. Place in a roasting tin without fat and sprinkle salt all over skin. Place in centre of oven and cook for calculated time. Pour off fat from tin during cooking.

4. To serve goose: Lift on to a warmed serving dish and remove trussing string. Place in oven with heat off and door ajar for 15 minutes before carving and while gravy and sugar-browned potatoes are being cooked and apples (for garnish) poached. Peel, halve and core apples and poach until tender in gently simmering water. Drain and arrange around goose. To cook the sugar-browned potatoes: Drain liquor from can of potatoes, but leave potatoes wet. Sprinkle sugar in a frying pan and place over a low heat to melt; when sugar turns a light golden brown, add butter. When bubbling, add potatoes. Shake pan gently to coat. Cook over a gentle heat for about 10 minutes; turn occasionally, until golden brown. Place in a warmed vegetable dish. Just before serving, place a teaspoonful of redcurrant jelly in each apple half and a bunch of watercress below tip of breastbone of goose. Serve with sugar-browned potatoes, sweet and sour red cabbage and gravy.

Note: Please see page 56 for the recipe for Sweet and Sour Red Cabbage, or use a 12¼oz jar of ready-to-serve Danish Red Cabbage.

Wienerbrød

(Danish Pastries)

These light, flaky delicacies originated about 100 years ago, when Copenhagen bakers went on strike for cash, instead of room and board. Employers retaliated by dismissing Danish bakers and importing Austrians to take their places. The Austrian method of folding butter into dough became popular, and when the Danish bakers eventually returned to their jobs they embellished the Austrians' method by adding jam, and other fillings to the variously-shaped pastries.

Makes 20:

YEAST LIQUID:

1 level teaspoon castor sugar
5 tablespoons hand-hot water (110 deg F)

2 level teaspoons dried yeast

DOUGH:

8oz plain flour
½ level teaspoon salt
1oz lard
1 level tablespoon castor sugar

1 standard egg, beaten
5oz butter

EGG GLAZE:

1 egg yolk
1 level teaspoon castor sugar

FILLINGS (see recipes):

Almond Paste
Apple and Raisin Filling

Spice Filling
(and 1oz currants, 1oz cut mixed peel)

DECORATION:

Glacé cherries
Glacé icing

Flaked browned almonds

1. Dissolve sugar in the water in a small basin. Sprinkle on yeast, then leave in a warm place until frothy, about 10 minutes.

2. Place flour and salt in a bowl. Add lard, cut into small pieces, and rub in with the fingertips. Add 1 level tablespoon castor sugar, beaten egg and yeast liquid, and mix with a fork to form a soft dough. Turn out on to a floured board and knead lightly until smooth. Wrap in foil or greased polythene and leave to rest in a cold place for 10 minutes.

3. Work the butter on a plate with a round-ended knife until soft (do not melt). Roll out dough to a 10in square. Spread butter in an oblong, 9in by 5in, in the centre of dough, ½in in from each side, and 2½in from each end. Fold the 2 unbuttered ends of dough over, so that they just overlap each other in the centre. Press edges with a rolling pin, to seal.

4. Turn dough and roll out to an oblong, about 15in by 5in. Fold dough, bringing top third over centre portion, then cover with lower third. Lift on to a plate, cover with foil or greased polythene and leave in a cold place for at least 10 minutes (in hot weather, leave for half an hour, or until butter is very firm). Repeat rolling, folding and resting the dough twice more.

5. Beat egg yolk, sugar and 1 tablespoon of water together.

6. To make pastries: Roll out half of dough and trim edges to make an oblong, 12in by 6in. Cut into 8 (3in) squares. Make 4 Stars and 4 Tivoli Pastries from these squares, as follows: To make Stars: Place a small ball of almond paste in the centre of each square. Cut each corner of the squares to within ½in of the centre and fold alternate points on to the almond paste, pressing centre tips firmly. Place a halved glacé cherry in centre of each. Place on a baking sheet.
To make Tivoli Pastries: Place a little Apple and Raisin Filling in an oblong across each square diagonally. Fold over two opposite corners, so that one overlaps the other in the centre, brushing underneath top corner with a little egg glaze, to make it stick. Place on a baking sheet.
To make Pinwheels: Roll out remaining pastry and trim edges to make an oblong, 14in by 6in. Spread with Spice Filling, the currants and the peel. Starting from a short edge, roll up, Swiss-roll fashion, and cut into 12 (½in) slices. Place on a baking sheet.

7. Prepare a hot oven (425 deg F, Gas Mark 7). Brush pastries with egg glaze; leave in a slightly warm place until puffy, about 25 minutes.

8. Bake the pastries for 10 to 15 minutes until golden brown. Ice with glacé icing while still hot, and decorate with flaked browned almonds.

Note: Alternatively, use fresh yeast: Blend ½oz with measured amount of warm water (omit 1 level teaspoon sugar) and use at once.

Almond Paste

2oz ground almonds
2oz castor sugar

1 to 2 drops almond essence
Egg white

Mix dry ingredients together. Stir in almond essence and sufficient egg white to bind to a soft paste. Use as required.

Apple and Raisin Filling

2oz stoned raisins
1 small cooking apple

1½oz demerara sugar

Chop raisins. Peel, quarter and core apple, and grate into a bowl. Stir in raisins and sugar. Use as required.

Spice Filling

1oz butter
1oz castor sugar

1 level teaspoon cinnamon

Place all ingredients in a bowl and cream with a wooden spoon until blended. Use as required.

The Cooking of Greece and Turkey

The cooking of these two countries is similar. In the warm Mediterranian climate, vegetables and fruits are very plentiful. Aubergines, vine leaves and peppers are often stuffed with rice or meat mixtures and served as a complete course. Olive oil is used a great deal in cooking, as is honey, which is produced in Greece. Honey is used instead of sugar in many recipes, particularly in the famous Greek pastries, such as Baclava.

As seas surround most of Greece, fish are plentiful, too. Shellfish, whitebait, mullet, mackerel and hake are all relatively cheap.

Rose water is frequently used in recipes in Turkey, particularly in the traditional rose petal jam and Turkish delight, which is very popular in Britain. Turkish kebabs are also well known in this country.

Greece

Moussaka

1

3

2

4

THE MEAT: Boneless lamb is required. Use neck fillet or a half shoulder, and ask your butcher to bone it. Best-quality minced beef could be used instead.

AUBERGINES: These are sometimes called Egg Plants; they give the dish a distinctive flavour. If aubergines are not available in your district, use marrow or cucumber. Alternatively, make a more substantial dish: omit aubergines, but put a layer of sliced raw potato below the meat and above tomato before covering with sauce.

ingredients

For 4 or 5 portions:
Half shoulder of lamb, boned (1½lb weight with bone) or 1lb boneless neck fillet
½lb onions
2 medium-sized aubergines
1lb tomatoes or 1 large (15½oz) can peeled tomatoes

2oz butter
Salt and pepper
2 level tablespoons chopped parsley
1 tablespoon olive oil

SAUCE:
1½oz margarine
1½oz plain flour
¾ pint milk
1½oz cheese, grated
1 standard egg, beaten

method **1.** Prepare a moderate oven (375 deg F, Gas Mark 5). Grease a 3-pint, shallow ovenproof dish. Cut lamb into ½in dice, removing any excess fat. Peel and slice onions. Slice aubergines. Skin and slice tomatoes. (Canned tomatoes should be drained in a sieve.)

2. Heat half the butter in a frying pan and gently fry onions to soften them, without browning. Add meat and continue frying gently, stirring, until meat changes colour. Remove from heat and stir in some salt and pepper. Spread meat mixture in ovenproof dish and sprinkle with parsley. Heat remaining butter and the olive oil (or omit oil and use an extra 1oz butter) in frying pan and fry aubergine slices on both sides, to brown lightly. (Add a little extra butter, if necessary.) Drain on kitchen paper.

3. Arrange aubergine slices on meat in dish; add some salt, then place tomatoes on top, adding a little more salt.

4. To make sauce: Melt margarine in a small saucepan, add flour, and cook for 2 minutes. Stir in milk and bring to boil, stirring; cook for 3 minutes. Remove from heat. Add grated cheese, together with the beaten egg. Taste and season with salt and pepper. Pour over layers in dish. Cover with lid, foil or greased greaseproof paper. Place on a baking sheet just above centre of oven for 1 hour. Remove lid or covering and cook for a further half hour. Serve hot with vegetables.

Note: Marrow or cucumber may be used instead of the aubergines. Marrow should be peeled, sliced and seeded. Cucumber should be peeled and sliced. Fry them as for aubergines. If desired, use 2lb of uncooked, sliced potatoes instead of aubergines. Start and finish the dish with a layer of raw potato slices, then top with sauce.

Psari Plaki

(Baked Fish)

'Psari' is the Greek word for fish. A great variety of fish is caught in the seas around Greece, so fish appears quite often on Greek menus. Plaki is the national fish dish, and mackerel, red mullet or hake can be used to make it.

For 4 portions:

4 medium-sized mackerel	1 lemon
Salt	1 tablespoon oil
2 large onions	Chopped parsley
½lb tomatoes	¼ level teaspoon pepper
1 clove of garlic	

1. Prepare a moderate oven (350 deg F, Gas Mark 4). Grease a shallow, ovenproof dish.
2. Cut off heads, tails and fins of mackerel, using a sharp knife. Slit each fish along underside and remove gut.
3. Wash mackerel in cold water; remove any black marks on the inside by rubbing with a little salt. Dry on kitchen paper and place in dish.
4. Peel and finely chop onions. Place tomatoes in a bowl and cover with boiling water. Leave for 1 minute, drain, then peel and chop. Peel clove of garlic and place on a saucer with 1 level teaspoon salt. Using a round-ended knife, rub salt against garlic to crush clove. Squeeze 1 tablespoon juice from 1 half of lemon; cut 3 thin slices from other half.
5. Heat oil in a frying pan; fry onion and garlic for 3 minutes, add tomatoes, 2 level teaspoons parsley, lemon juice and pepper and cook for 2 minutes. Pour over fish and place dish in centre of oven. Bake for 20 to 25 minutes, until fish is cooked.
6. To serve, sprinkle with chopped parsley; cut lemon slices through to centre, twist and arrange on top of fish.

Taramasalata

(Smoked Cod's Roe Pâté)
(pictured on back cover)

Taramasalata is traditionally served in Greece with bread, as a first course to a meal. It can also be served on toast for parties.

For 4 snack or first-course portions:

4oz smoked cod's roe	Pepper
⅛ pint olive oil	1 level teaspoon chopped
2oz mashed potato or 1oz	chives or grated onion
white breadcrumbs	1 level tablespoon chopped
1 tablespoon lemon juice	parsley

1. Remove skin from cod's roe; place roe in a basin with 1 tablespoon of the measured olive oil. Leave to soften for 5 minutes.
2. Sieve roe, then potato into a bowl. (If using breadcrumbs, place in a basin, cover with cold water, then place in a sieve and press with a small saucer or base of a bowl to extract as much water as possible; add to cod's roe.) Mix well.
3. Gradually beat in remaining oil, a teaspoonful at a time.
4. Add lemon juice, pepper, chives or onion and parsley (the chives can be cut finely with scissors) and mix thoroughly. The mixture will have the consistency of a creamed cake mix. Pile into a small dish and serve with bread or crisp rolls, salad and olives.

Note: Taramasalata may be made in an electric liquidiser. Place skinned cod's roe, oil and lemon juice in liquidiser goblet and run machine until mixture is smooth. Place in a basin and add sieved potato or soaked breadcrumbs, pepper, chives or onion and parsley.

Imam Baïldi

(Stuffed Aubergines)

Green and red peppers, aubergines, courgettes and artichokes are the everyday vegetables grown in Turkey.

For 4 portions:

2 medium-sized aubergines	½ level teaspoon salt
2 large tomatoes	2 tablespoons oil
1 small onion	1oz white breadcrumbs
1 small green pepper	Pepper
2 cloves of garlic	

1. Prepare a moderate oven (350 deg F, Gas Mark 4).
2. Remove stalks from aubergines. Place aubergines in a large saucepan; cover with water. Bring to boil, cover and simmer for 5 minutes; drain. Cut aubergines in halves lengthwise. Scoop out flesh and chop; place aubergine shells in a shallow, ovenproof dish.
3. Place tomatoes in a bowl and cover with boiling water. Leave for 1 minute, drain, then peel and chop. Peel and chop onion. Cut pepper in half lengthwise; discard core, seeds and white pith. Chop pepper. Peel cloves of garlic and place on a saucer with salt. Using a round-ended knife, rub salt against garlic to crush cloves.
4. Heat oil in a frying pan, add chopped aubergines, onion, green pepper and garlic and fry for 5 minutes. Stir in tomatoes, breadcrumbs and a little pepper; mix well together.
5. Fill aubergine shells with stuffing; cover with a buttered paper and cook in oven for 30 to 40 minutes.
6. Serve hot as a vegetable, or cold as a first course.

Shish Kebab

For centuries, the Turks have been grilling pieces of meat on skewers. They usually serve the kebabs with a pilaff.

For 4 portions:

1lb boned leg of lamb	8 small onions

MARINADE:

1 small onion	1 level teaspoon salt
4 tablespoons tarragon or	1 level tablespoon chopped
wine vinegar	parsley
8 tablespoons oil	½ level teaspoon mixed
½ level teaspoon pepper	dried herbs

PILAFF:

1 chicken stock cube
1 pint boiling water
1 large tomato
1oz margarine

6oz short-grain rice
1 level teaspoon salt
Pepper

GARNISH:

Parsley

1. Remove excess fat from meat; cut meat into 1in dice.

2. Peel 8 onions; place in a saucepan, cover with cold water and bring to boil. Cover and simmer for 5 minutes; drain, rinse in cold water and cut into halves.

3. Make marinade: Peel and very finely chop onion; place in a basin. Add the remaining marinade ingredients and mix well. Place lamb in basin and leave in a cool place for at least 3 hours giving an occasional stir.

4. Make pilaff: Dissolve stock cube in boiling water. Place tomato in a bowl and cover with boiling water. Leave for 1 minute, drain, then peel and chop.

5. Melt margarine in a saucepan, add rice and fry for 2 minutes; add chopped tomato, stock, salt and a little pepper. Bring to boil, cover, and simmer for 20 minutes, or until rice is cooked and has absorbed stock.

6. Prepare a moderate grill. Thread meat on to 4 skewers, alternating pieces of meat with an onion half. Brush grill rack with a little oil.

7. Brush food on skewers with marinade. Place on grill rack; grill for 10 to 15 minutes, turning once, and basting with a little marinade occasionally.

8. Place pilaff on a warmed serving dish and arrange kebabs on top. Garnish each kebab with a sprig of parsley. Serve immediately.

Stifado

(Beef and Onion Stew)

This is one of the many stews that are made in Greece. Stifado has an unusual flavour and is ideal to serve at a party, as it can be prepared in advance and reheated.

For 4 portions:

1lb stewing steak
2 cloves of garlic
1 level teaspoon salt
1lb button onions or shallots
1 tablespoon oil

1 (5½oz) can tomato purée
⅛ pint red wine
2 bay leaves
½ level teaspoon ground cinnamon

1. Cut meat into 1in dice. Peel cloves of garlic and place on a saucer with salt. Using a round-ended knife, rub salt against garlic to crush cloves. Peel onions or shallots.

2. Heat oil in a large saucepan, fry meat, onions and garlic for 5 minutes. Add tomato purée, red wine, bay leaves and cinnamon; bring to boil, cover, and gently simmer for 2½ to 3 hours until meat is tender.

3. Remove bay leaves and turn out stew into a warmed serving dish. Serve with a pilaff (see recipe above).

Dolmades

(Stuffed Vine Leaves)

This dish is served in both Greece and Turkey, the Turkish name being Dolma. An alternative filling is a rice stuffing, which would be served on the days that the Greeks do not eat meat or fish. Vine leaves are available in packets from grocery stores specialising in Greek foods; cabbage leaves make a very satisfactory alternative.

For 4 portions:

Vine leaves or cabbage leaves
1 small onion
1 beef stock cube
Boiling water
1 tablespoon oil
8oz minced beef
2oz short-grain rice

2 level teaspoons chopped parsley
1 level teaspoon salt
¼ level teaspoon pepper
1 tablespoon lemon juice
3 level tablespoons tomato purée

1. Prepare a moderate oven (350 deg F, Gas Mark 4). Wash vine or cabbage leaves, if necessary. Cook in boiling water for 2 minutes, then drain.

2. Peel and finely chop onion. Dissolve stock cube in ½ pint boiling water.

3. Heat oil in a medium-sized saucepan; add minced beef and onion and fry for 3 minutes. Stir in rice, parsley, salt and pepper; cook for 2 minutes. Add stock and lemon juice; bring to boil, cover and simmer for 20 minutes or until rice has absorbed stock.

4. Place a little meat mixture inside each vine or cabbage leaf and wrap leaves around; tuck ends under neatly (if necessary, tie with fine string or cotton) and place in a shallow, ovenproof dish.

5. Mix tomato purée with ½ pint boiling water; pour over stuffed leaves. Cover dish with a lid or foil; place in oven and cook for 1 hour. Remove string, if used, and serve hot with mashed potato.

Greece

Loukoumades (Honey Puffs)

1

3

2

4

THE DOUGH: The basic enriched bread dough is used for the puffs; they are rolled into balls and fried like doughnuts. If time is short, use a baking powder doughnut recipe. Roll out the dough and cut into rounds with a small cutter. THE SAUCE: The sweetness of honey is balanced by the tartness of the lemon juice to make a delicious rich sauce. The sauce is thickened with custard powder, and must be completed just before serving, because it becomes thinner if stored.

ingredients

For 4 portions:
YEAST BATTER:

2oz plain flour
2 level teaspoons dried
or ½oz fresh yeast.
1 level teaspoon honey
¼ pint hand-hot milk

DOUGH:

6oz plain flour
½ level teaspoon salt
1oz margarine

SAUCE:

1½ tablespoons lemon juice
2 level tablespoons custard powder
8oz granulated sugar
4 level tablespoons thick honey

Oil or lard for deep frying
1 rounded tablespoon granulated sugar
½ level teaspoon ground cinnamon
1oz blanched almonds

method

1. Place batter ingredients in a large bowl. Beat well with a wooden spoon until smooth, then leave in a warm place until frothy, about 20 minutes. Place dough ingredients in a bowl. Cut fat into small pieces and rub in with the fingertips until the mixture resembles fine breadcrumbs. Add to batter; mix well with a wooden spoon or with the hands.

2. Turn out on to a lightly-floured board. Knead and stretch dough by folding towards you, then pushing away with the palm of the hand. Give dough a quarter turn and repeat, developing a rocking motion. Knead for about 10 minutes until dough feels firm and elastic and no longer sticky. Place dough in a greased polythene bag and leave to rise in a warm place, until doubled in size and until dough springs back when pressed with a floured finger, about 45 minutes.

3. Turn out dough on to a floured board and divide into 20 pieces; shape into balls and place on a greased baking sheet. Cover with greased polythene and leave in a warm place until dough has doubled in size. While dough is rising, make sauce: Blend lemon juice and custard powder in a saucepan. Add ½ pint water and sugar; bring to boil, stirring, and simmer for 3 minutes. Cover and keep hot. Add honey just before serving.

4. Heat a pan of oil or lard to 370 deg F, or until a 1in cube of day-old bread browns in 40 seconds. Mix sugar and cinnamon on a plate. Place half the dough balls in the frying basket. Lower gently into pan and fry until golden brown all over. Remove from pan and roll doughnuts in cinnamon sugar. Keep them hot on kitchen paper while remainder are fried and coated. Pile on a hot dish, decorate with blanched almonds and serve hot with honey and lemon sauce.

Note: Double quantity of dough and batter mixture may be made up and half of it made into 8 plain doughnuts.

Adjhem Pilavi
(Lamb Pilaff)

The Turks are said to have introduced rice from Persia and this is the main ingredient used in pilaffs, for which they are renowned.

For 4 portions:

1lb boned, middle neck of lamb
1 small onion
1 small (8oz) can peeled tomatoes
Boiling water
1 beef stock cube
1 tablespoon oil
6oz short-grain rice
1oz currants
½ level teaspoon mixed spice
½ level teaspoon salt
¼ level teaspoon pepper
Chopped parsley

1. Remove any excess fat or gristle from lamb; cut lamb into small pieces. Peel and finely chop onion.

2. Drain can of tomatoes, reserving liquor. Chop tomatoes and make up tomato liquor to 1½ pints with boiling water. Add stock cube and stir until dissolved.

3. Heat oil in a large saucepan and fry lamb and onions for 5 minutes, turning occasionally. Stir in rice and cook for 2 minutes to allow rice to absorb fat. Add stock, currants, tomatoes, mixed spice, salt and pepper. Bring to boil, cover and simmer gently for 1 hour or until rice has absorbed stock and meat is tender; stir occasionally.

4. Place pilaff in a warmed serving dish and sprinkle with chopped parsley.

Lati-lokum
(Turkish Delight)

Makes about 30 pieces:

1oz blanched almonds
8oz granulated sugar
⅛ level teaspoon cream of tartar
1¾oz cornflour
4oz icing sugar
2 teaspoons rose water

COATING:
½oz icing sugar
½oz cornflour

1. Thoroughly grease a 5½in square tin. Finely chop blanched almonds.

2. Place granulated sugar and ¼ pint water in a medium-sized, heavy-based saucepan. Stir over a moderate heat until sugar has dissolved. Bring to boil and cook, without stirring, for 7 to 10 minutes until 'soft ball' stage is reached (240 deg F on a sugar thermometer or until a little of the syrup, when dropped in cold water, forms a soft ball).

3. Sprinkle cream of tartar on to syrup.

4. While syrup is cooking, mix cornflour and icing sugar smoothly with 4 tablespoons of cold water and put ½ pint of water on to heat in another saucepan.

5. Stir cornflour mixture into the hot water and boil for 3 minutes, stirring continuously.

6. Gradually add syrup to cooked cornflour mixture, beating well, and boil for 10 minutes, stirring continuously. Mixture should be a pale straw colour and translucent.

7. Stir in rose water and chopped almonds; pour into tin and leave to set.

8. Sieve icing sugar and cornflour together on to a board; cut Turkish Delight into squares and coat each piece with cornflour and icing sugar mixture. Pack into a box and sprinkle in between each layer with cornflour and icing sugar mixture.

Galaktoboyrekon
(Custard Cream Slices)

For 5 or 6 portions:
FILLING:

2 level tablespoons custard powder
1½ level tablespoons granulated sugar
¾ pint milk
1 large egg
1 teaspoon vanilla essence

SYRUP:

2oz granulated sugar
3 level tablespoons clear honey
1 tablespoon lemon juice
1oz butter
1 large (13oz) packet frozen puff pastry, just thawed

1. Prepare a hot oven (425 deg F, Gas Mark 7).

2. Make filling: Place custard powder and sugar in a basin. Blend with a little of the measured milk and put remaining milk on to heat. Add egg and vanilla essence to mixed custard powder and beat well together.

3. When milk is nearly boiling, pour on to mixed custard powder. Return to the pan, reduce heat to low, and bring slowly to boil, stirring continuously. Cook for 4 minutes, stirring; remove from heat. Place a piece of wetted grease-proof paper on custard to prevent a skin forming; leave until cold.

4. To make syrup: Dissolve sugar in ⅛ pint water, bring to boil, reduce heat and boil for 5 minutes. Remove from heat and stir in honey and lemon juice; leave to cool.

5. Melt butter in a saucepan over a low heat; brush bottom and sides of a 10in by 6½in shallow tin with melted butter.

6. Divide pastry in 2; roll out 1 piece to an oblong, 11in by 7½in, and line base and sides of tin. Dampen edges of pastry. Spread filling over pastry in tin. Roll out remaining pastry to an oblong, 10½in by 7in; lift over rolling pin on to filling. Seal pastry edges well and lightly score cuts diagonally across pastry. Brush with remaining melted butter and bake above centre of oven for about 25 minutes, until well risen and golden brown.

7. Pour syrup over pastry and carefully lift on to a warmed serving dish. Serve hot or cold.

The Cooking of Russia and Poland,

At one time, Poland was part of Russia, which explains why many of their recipes are similar. As Russia covers so vast an area, the climate, customs and cooking vary throughout the different regions. Over the centuries, Russian cooking has been influenced by many countries. Smetana (soured cream) is used in many recipes, giving a unique flavour to the dishes. Caviar is one of the best known foods that are exported from Russia. Soup is served very often by the Polish housewife. The Russian Borsch soup has been adapted and is now a Polish national dish, called Barszcz. The main ingredient is beetroot, which gives a good colour. Herrings, potatoes, cabbage and mushrooms, plentiful in Poland, are used in many Polish dishes.

Russia

Beef Stroganoff

1

2

3

4

SOURED OR CULTURED CREAM: This gives the dish its special flavour and richness. It is single cream that has been 'set', like yoghourt, with lactic acid bacillus, and imparts a slightly sharp and refreshing flavour to both sweet and savoury dishes. This cream is relatively inexpensive and is available from most dairies. Alternatively, you can sour single cream by adding a teaspoonful of lemon juice to a 5 fluid oz carton.

RICE: Use good-quality, long-grain rice. For parties, this can be cooked in advance, if desired. After draining the rice, spread in a baking tin lined with oiled greaseproof paper, allowing sufficient to cover over rice. One hour before serving, place in a cold oven, turn to cool setting (300 deg F, Gas Mark 2) and heat for 1 hour.

ingredients

For 4 portions:
1lb topside or rump steak
1 level teaspoon salt
Pepper
2 small onions
4oz mushrooms
2oz butter
1 rounded teaspoon
plain flour

1 rounded teaspoon
tomato purée
¼ pint stock or
¼ pint boiling water
and ½ beef stock cube
8oz long-grain rice
1 (5 fluid oz) carton
soured or cultured cream
Chopped parsley

method

1. Beat meat well with a rolling pin; trim off any excess fat. Cut across grain of meat into ¼in strips; cut strips into 1in lengths. Place on a plate and sprinkle with salt and some pepper. Peel and slice onions. Wash and slice mushrooms.

2. Melt butter in a saucepan; add onions and mushrooms and fry for 4 minutes, stirring occasionally. Add meat and fry for a further 5 minutes. Stir in flour and cook gently for about 2 minutes.

3. Add tomato purée and stock. Bring to boil, stirring continuously; cover and simmer for 15 minutes. Cook rice in a large saucepan containing at least 3 pints of boiling, salted water for about 12 minutes. Test by pressing a grain between thumb and finger; drain through a sieve or colander and rinse with hot water. Arrange the rice on a warmed serving dish.

4. Stir soured cream into beef; pour over rice and sprinkle with chopped parsley. Serve immediately with green salad.

Bigos

(Polish Hunter's Stew)

This is one of the oldest traditional Polish dishes. In former days it was served at royal banquets and hunts where it was a rich and elaborate dish. Nowadays, it is a more simply-made dish, cooked in the oven, and is very popular served in the cold winters of Poland.

For 6 portions:

½lb cabbage	1 beef stock cube
Salt	1 pint boiling water
1 medium-sized onion	1 (14oz) can sauerkraut
1 medium-sized cooking apple	2oz lard
	1oz flour
½lb cooked chicken, pork, veal or beef	2 rounded tablespoons tomato purée
¼lb streaky bacon	¼ pint red wine
¼lb Polish boiling sausage	Pepper
2oz mushrooms	1 bay leaf

1. Prepare a cool oven (325 deg F, Gas Mark 3). Cut off excess stalk and wash cabbage thoroughly. Discard any tough outside leaves and shred finely.

2. Bring ½ pint of water to boil in a large saucepan. Add 1 level teaspoon of salt. Add shredded cabbage and cook for 5 minutes; drain well in a colander.

3. Peel and chop onion. Peel, core and slice apple; place slices in cold, salted water to prevent browning.

4. Cut cooked meat into pieces. Remove rind and bone from bacon; cut bacon into strips. Remove skin and slice sausage. Wash and slice mushrooms. Dissolve stock cube in boiling water. Drain sauerkraut.

5. Melt lard in a saucepan, stir in chopped onion and bacon; fry until onion is golden brown. Stir in flour and cook gently for about 2 minutes. Add tomato purée, stock and wine; bring to boil, stirring continuously. Add ¼ level teaspoon salt, some pepper and bay leaf.

6. Layer sauerkraut, cabbage, meat, apple, sausage and mushrooms in a 4-pint casserole. Pour gravy over, cover and cook in centre of oven for 2 hours; remove bay leaf. Serve with boiled potatoes and a green vegetable.

Note: This dish improves if cooled quickly, stored in a cool place and reheated on the following day.

Kulichs

(Bird Cakes)

Kulich, which means bird cake, is traditionally served at Easter time in Russia.

Makes 8:

BATTER:

5 tablespoons warm milk	½oz fresh yeast or 2 level teaspoons dried yeast
2oz plain flour	
½oz castor sugar	

DOUGH:

1oz blanched almonds	½ level teaspoon salt
6oz plain flour	1 standard egg
1oz currants	3 tablespoons oil
2oz castor sugar	½ teaspoon vanilla essence

DECORATION:

½oz blanched almonds	2oz icing sugar
2 glacé cherries	Hot water

1. Grease 8 castle pudding (dariole) tins. Place batter ingredients in a large bowl. Beat well with a wooden spoon until smooth; set aside in a warm place until frothy, about 30 minutes.

2. Chop 1oz almonds. Mix with 6oz flour, currants, sugar and salt in a bowl. Beat egg in a small basin.

3. Add flour mixture, egg, oil and vanilla essence to batter; mix well with a wooden spoon. Turn out on to a lightly-floured board and knead and stretch dough, by folding towards you, then pushing away with the palm of the hand. Give dough a quarter turn and repeat, developing a rocking motion. Knead for about 10 minutes, until dough feels firm and elastic.

4. Place dough in a lightly floured bowl. Cover with greased polythene or foil; leave to rise in a warm place until doubled in size and until dough springs back when pressed with a floured finger, about 1 hour.

5. Turn out dough on to lightly floured board and knead for 1 to 2 minutes.

6. Cut dough into 8 pieces, shape into balls and press dough into tins.

7. Cover tins with greased polythene or foil and leave until dough has risen to top of tins. Remove polythene.

8. Prepare a moderate oven (375 deg F, Gas Mark 5). Bake in centre of oven for 20 to 25 minutes until golden brown. Turn out and leave to cool on a wire rack.

9. Chop ½oz almonds and glacé cherries. Sieve icing sugar into a bowl; beat in sufficient hot water to allow icing to thickly coat back of a spoon. Coat cakes with icing and sprinkle with almonds and cherries.

The Cooking of The Orient

Curries are to India as stews are to Britain, and they vary according to the region and the spices used. Madrassi curries are more pungent and thinner than the Hindustani ones. Bengalis specialise in fish and bamboo shoot curries.

Ground chilli and ginger are used to flavour the hot curries—coriander and cummin seeds the mild, aromatic ones. The quantity of chilli or curry powder can be varied to taste.

In Indonesia, rice is often eaten three times a day with fish, chicken, meat and vegetables, served in a variety of ways. Piquancy is added by sauces which accompany the various dishes. No pungent spices are used in Chinese cookery, and the vegetables and meat are chopped finely and cooked rapidly, thus retaining crispness. Several dishes are served at a time, with boiled rice, fried rice and crispy noodles.

India

Chicken Curry

1

3

2

4

Curry sauce is made from onions, garlic and spices. Most stewing meats, poultry and some vegetables can be curried.

SPICES: Indians grind the spices for their curries, but unless you make curry frequently, it is more convenient to buy them in small quantities already ground. Always measure spices accurately. Chilli and ginger make a curry hot, so add these sparingly at first. Spices and ingredients for curry, including poppadums, are obtainable in high-class grocery and oriental stores.

SIDE DISHES: These are served to complement the flavour of the curry and are crisp, sweet, sour, bland or refreshing.

Serve 4 to 6 of the following:

POPPADUMS: These are large, round and paper thin. They are cooked by frying on each side for a second or two, or by grilling quickly. They puff up when cooked and are crumbled over the curry.

CHUTNEY: Mango chutney gives the right sweet and sour flavour for serving with curry.

SLICED BANANAS: Toss these in lemon juice to prevent discoloration.

Natural yoghourt, pineapple chunks, thickly-sliced cucumber and sliced tomatoes are refreshing with hot curries.

ingredients

For 4 portions:

CURRY SPICE MIX:

2 cloves
¼ to ½ level teaspoon ground ginger

1 level teaspoon turmeric
1½ level teaspoons ground coriander
1 level teaspoon ground cummin seed
¼ level teaspoon cinnamon
¼ to ½ level teaspoon chilli powder

¾ lb onions
4 cloves of garlic
2 level teaspoons salt
¾ lb tomatoes
4 chicken joints

2 tablespoons oil
1 level tablespoon plain flour
½ pint stock or water
8oz long-grain rice

method

1. Crush cloves between 2 teaspoons and place on a plate. Carefully measure spices, levelling off each spoon with a knife, and add to cloves. Peel and slice onions. Peel cloves of garlic and place on a saucer with the salt. Using a round-ended knife, rub salt against the garlic to crush cloves. Place tomatoes in a bowl and cover with boiling water. Leave for about 1 minute, drain, then peel and chop. Halve chicken joints.

2. Heat oil in a large saucepan and fry spices for 2 minutes. Add chicken joints and fry until brown. Remove from saucepan on to a plate.

3. Fry onion and garlic until soft, then stir in flour and tomatoes and cook for about 2 minutes. Return chicken joints to saucepan. Stir in stock or water, bring to boil, stirring, then cover and simmer for about 2 hours until sauce is reduced to a thick gravy.

4. Cook rice in a large saucepan containing at least 3 pints of boiling, salted water for about 12 minutes. Test by pressing a grain between thumb and finger; drain and rinse with boiling water. Arrange rice on a warmed serving dish, with chicken on top and curry sauce poured over. Serve with poppadums, sliced bananas tossed in lemon juice, pineapple chunks, sliced cucumber, mango chutney, sliced tomatoes.

Note: The curry improves in flavour if made the day before it is required. Use the larger quantity of ginger and chilli powder for a hot curry.

75

To Cook Long-grain Rice

Cook rice in a large saucepan of boiling, salted water for about 12 minutes. Test by pressing a grain between thumb and finger. Drain and rinse with hot water. Use immediately or line a baking tin with oiled greaseproof paper, allowing sufficient to fold over tin. Spread rice in tin and cover with paper. Place in a cool oven (300 deg F, Gas Mark 2) for about half an hour or until required. To keep rice hot for more than 1 hour, place in a very cool oven (275 deg F, Gas Mark 1).

Curried Vegetables

For 4 portions:

1 onion	1 chicken stock cube
1½lb mixed vegetables	1 pint boiling water
(carrots, parsnips, turnips,	1 rounded tablespoon
potatoes, celery, leeks)	mango chutney
1oz margarine	1oz sultanas
2 level tablespoons curry	Squeeze of lemon juice
powder	8oz long-grain rice
1 level tablespoon plain	Salt and pepper
flour	

1. Peel and chop onion. Peel and finely slice carrots. Peel other root vegetables and cut into ¼in dice; wash and slice celery and leeks.

2. Melt margarine in a medium-sized saucepan. Add onion and curry powder; fry for 3 minutes. Add remaining vegetables and flour and cook for 3 minutes, stirring.

3. Dissolve stock cube in boiling water and add to saucepan with mango chutney, sultanas and lemon juice. Bring to boil, stirring; cover and simmer for 30 to 35 minutes, until vegetables are tender.

4. Cook long-grain rice (see recipe). Arrange around the edge of a large, warmed serving dish.

5. Taste curry and season with some salt and pepper, if necessary; arrange in centre of rice.

Note: For a vegetarian dish, replace chicken stock cube with yeast extract, or use vegetable stock or water.

Koaftah Beef Curry

Koaftahs are balls of meat or fish, which are cooked in a moderately hot, spicy curry sauce.

For 4 to 6 portions:

2 onions	¼ level teaspoon ground
2 cloves of garlic	turmeric
1 level teaspoon salt	½ level teaspoon ground
1½lb minced beef	ginger
3 level tablespoons fresh	½ level teaspoon freshly-
white breadcrumbs	ground black pepper
1 standard egg	1 beef stock cube
1 level teaspoon mixed	½ pint boiling water
dried herbs	8oz long-grain rice
2oz lard	2 rounded teaspoons
1 level teaspoon chilli	cornflour
powder	

1. Peel and thinly slice onions. Peel cloves of garlic and place on a saucer with salt. Using a round-ended knife, rub salt against garlic to crush cloves.

2. Place minced beef, breadcrumbs, egg and mixed dried herbs into a bowl; mix well with a fork. Divide mixture into 20 pieces; roll into balls with floured hands.

3. Melt lard in a large saucepan. Add meatballs and fry until browned; remove from pan. Add onion and garlic to fat in saucepan and fry until onion is soft; stir in chilli powder, turmeric, ground ginger and black pepper; fry for 2 minutes.

4. Dissolve stock cube in boiling water; add to saucepan. Bring to boil, return meatballs to saucepan, cover and simmer for 1¼ to 1½ hours.

5. Cook long-grain rice (see recipe). Arrange rice on a warmed serving dish.

6. Blend cornflour with a little cold water. Add to curry and bring to boil, stirring; cook for 2 minutes. Arrange meatballs on rice and pour curry sauce over. Serve immediately.

Beef Vindaloo or Bindaloo

This is a hot, spicy curry; it is thought to have originated from the Portuguese settlers in India.

For 6 portions:

2 onions	1 bay leaf
2 cloves of garlic	1 level teaspoon freshly-
1 to 2 level teaspoons salt	ground black pepper
2lb stewing steak	2oz butter
¼ pint vinegar	
4 level tablespoons curry	
powder	

1. Peel and thinly slice onions. Peel cloves of garlic and place on a saucer with salt. Using a round-ended knife, rub salt against the garlic to crush cloves. Remove any fat from stewing steak; cut meat into 1in dice.

2. Place onion, garlic and meat in a bowl. Add vinegar, curry powder, bay leaf and black pepper to bowl; turn until well mixed. Cover and leave in a cold place or refrigerator for 24 hours or overnight.

3. Melt butter in a large saucepan. Add meat mixture and cook for 2 to 3 minutes. Stir in ¼ pint of water. Bring to boil, cover and simmer for 2 hours or until meat is tender. Taste and add more salt and pepper, if necessary. Remove bay leaf. Serve with boiled, long-grain rice (see recipe).

Note: This curry improves in flavour if cooled quickly and kept in a cold place overnight.

Prawn Pilau

Pilau was originally an Arabian dish and can also be made with chicken, lamb or beef.

For 4 portions:

2 onions	6 peppercorns
4 cardamoms	4 level tablespoons
6 cloves	desiccated coconut

½ pint boiling water
8oz long-grain rice
4oz butter or margarine
Pinch of ground cinnamon

1 to 2 level teaspoons salt
2oz sultanas
6oz shelled prawns

GARNISH:
2 hard-boiled eggs

1. Peel and slice onions lengthwise. Break outer shell of cardamoms and remove seeds; discard shells. Crush cardamom seeds, cloves and peppercorns with the back of a wooden spoon.

2. Place coconut in a jug and add boiling water. Leave for 15 minutes; strain, reserving liquor. Place rice in a sieve and wash thoroughly; drain.

3. Melt butter or margarine in a medium-sized saucepan. Add onions and fry until golden brown. Add rice and cook for 1 minute. Add cardamom seeds, cloves, peppercorns, cinnamon, salt, coconut liquor and 1 pint water. Bring to boil, cover and simmer for 10 to 12 minutes, stirring occasionally, until rice is tender and liquid is absorbed.

4. Add sultanas and prawns and cook, stirring, for a further 3 minutes.

5. Turn pilau out into a warmed serving dish. Arrange hard-boiled eggs, cut into quarters, around edge of dish. Serve immediately.

Chicken Birianee

A mild aromatic curry.

For 8 portions:
1lb long-grain rice
8 chicken joints
3 onions
1 clove of garlic
1oz coriander seeds
2 level teaspoons salt
8oz margarine

1 level teaspoon turmeric
1oz ground cummin seeds
1 level tablespoon freshly-ground black pepper
3oz sultanas
3oz raisins
2oz salted almonds

1. Wash rice and leave in a bowl of cold water for 1 to 2 hours; drain. Wash and trim chicken joints. Peel onions and cut in halves; peel clove of garlic.

2. Place chicken joints, onions and garlic in a large saucepan. Add 3 pints cold water, coriander seeds and salt. Bring to boil, cover and simmer for 1 hour, or until the chicken joints are tender.

3. Lift out chicken joints with a draining spoon; remove skin from chicken joints. Strain chicken stock, reserving 2 pints and the onions; wash saucepan.

4. Melt margarine in saucepan. Add cooked onions and fry until well browned. Stir in rice, turmeric, cummin seeds, black pepper and reserved 2 pints chicken stock. Bring to boil, add chicken joints, sultanas and half the raisins; cover and simmer for 8 to 10 minutes, until rice is tender and all stock is absorbed. Taste and add more salt, if necessary.

5. Turn out mixture into a large serving dish. Sprinkle with salted almonds and remaining raisins.

Haddock and Tuna Curry

A moderately hot aromatic curry.

For 4 portions:
1 large onion
½lb young carrots
1 clove of garlic
Salt
¾lb haddock fillet
2 tablespoons oil
2 level teaspoons curry paste
2 level teaspoons curry powder

1 level tablespoon plain flour
1 large (15½oz) can butter beans
1 (7oz) can tuna steak
1 tablespoon malt vinegar
8oz long-grain rice
Pepper

1. Peel and thinly slice onion. Scrape carrots and thinly slice. Peel clove of garlic and place on a saucer with a little salt. Using a round-ended knife, rub salt against the garlic to crush clove. Wash haddock and remove skin; cut haddock into small pieces.

2. Place onion, carrots, garlic, oil, curry paste and curry powder together in a saucepan and fry for 5 minutes, stirring occasionally. Add flour and cook for 1 minute. Add haddock, contents of cans of butter beans and tuna, ¼ pint water and vinegar. Bring slowly to boil, stirring gently; cover and simmer for 15 minutes, until fish is tender.

3. Cook long-grain rice (see recipe). Place in a warmed serving dish.

4. Taste curry and season with some salt and pepper, if necessary. Serve with rice and other accompaniments (see page 75).

Dhall

(Indian Lentils)

This lentil dish is especially popular in the Punjab, where it is served as an accompaniment to curries.

For 6 to 8 portions:
1 medium-sized onion
8oz lentils
2oz butter or margarine
½ level teaspoon chilli powder

½ level teaspoon turmeric
1 chicken stock cube
Boiling water
Salt

1. Peel and chop onion. Place lentils in a sieve and wash thoroughly.

2. Melt butter or margarine in a medium-sized saucepan. Add onion and fry for 2 to 3 minutes, until tender. Stir in chilli powder and turmeric and cook for 1 minute; add lentils. Dissolve stock cube in 1½ pints boiling water and add to pan. Bring to boil, cover and simmer for 1 to 1¼ hours, until lentils are tender and stock is absorbed, stirring occasionally and adding a little extra boiling water, if necessary. Taste and season with salt, if necessary. Serve hot with curries.

China

Crispy Noodles
Prawns with Mixed Vegetables

Crispy Pancake Rolls
Sweet and Sour Pork Balls

Crispy Noodles

Prawns with Mixed Vegetables

Crispy Pancake Rolls

Sweet and Sour Pork Balls

Most ingredients used in Chinese cookery are available in large food stores or oriental shops.

SOY SAUCE: Gives a spicy flavour.

WATER CHESTNUTS: Bland and very crisp. They are available in cans.

BEAN SPROUTS: Also available in cans, but texture is better if you can buy them fresh.

NOODLES: Can be made at home; alternatively, use ribbon egg noodles.

PRAWN CRACKERS: Sometimes called shrimp slices, are deep fried for a few seconds in hot fat. They puff up quickly, but should not brown.

Prawns with Mixed Vegetables

For 4 to 6 portions (with other Chinese dishes):
1 golden meat extract cube, ¼ pint boiling water, 1 large carrot, 2in piece of cucumber, half a 10oz can water chestnuts, 1 tablespoon oil, 3 level teaspoons cornflour, ¼ level teaspoon sugar, 3oz bean sprouts, fresh or canned, 4oz peeled prawns

method

1. Dissolve meat extract cube in the boiling water. Peel carrot. Cut carrot and cucumber into strips. Slice water chestnuts.

2. Heat oil in a saucepan and fry carrot, cucumber and water chestnuts for 3 minutes without browning. Stir in cornflour, stock and sugar; bring to boil, stirring, cover and simmer for 3 minutes.

3. Add bean sprouts and prawns; cover and simmer for 3 minutes. Pour into a warmed dish and serve.

Sweet and Sour Pork Balls

For 4 to 6 portions (with other Chinese dishes):
SAUCE: *1 medium-sized onion, half a green pepper, ½oz margarine, 2 rounded teaspoons cornflour, 2 level tablespoons chutney, 3 level teaspoons tomato purée, 2 teaspoons soy sauce, 2 level teaspoons castor sugar, 1 tablespoon vinegar. 4oz to 6oz lean pork.* BATTER: *3oz self-raising flour, half a standard egg, ½ teaspoon oil for batter, oil or lard for deep frying*

method

1. Peel and slice onion. Discard seeds, core and white pith from green pepper and slice into strips.

2. Fry onion in margarine in a saucepan for 3 minutes without browning. Stir in cornflour, chutney, tomato purée, soy sauce, sugar, vinegar, ½ pint water and green pepper. Bring to boil, stirring; cover and simmer for 10 minutes.

3. Cut pork into 1in dice. Make batter: Measure ¼ pint water. Place flour in a basin, make a 'well' in centre and add egg, about half the measured water and ½ teaspoon oil. Beat until smooth; blend in remaining water. Heat a pan of oil or lard to 370 deg F or until a 1in cube of day-old bread browns in 40 seconds. Dip pork cubes in batter and fry for 5 minutes until golden brown and crisp; drain on kitchen paper. Pour sauce into a hot serving dish and arrange crispy pork on top. Serve immediately.

Please turn to next page for recipes for Crispy Noodles and Crispy Pancake Rolls.

Crispy Pancake Rolls

For 4 to 6 portions (with other Chinese dishes):

FILLING:

1 medium-sized onion
1 chicken joint
1oz mushrooms
1 tablespoon oil
½ level teaspoon salt
½ level teaspoon pepper

½ level teaspoon castor sugar
1 teaspoon soy sauce
3oz bean sprouts, fresh or canned

BATTER:

1 standard egg
Oil or lard for shallow and deep frying

4oz plain flour

1. Peel and chop onion. Discard skin from chicken joint; cut off meat and dice. Wash and chop mushrooms.

2. Heat 1 tablespoon oil in a saucepan and gently fry onion, chicken and mushrooms for 2 to 3 minutes. Add salt, pepper, sugar, soy sauce and bean sprouts; mix well and remove from heat.

3. Place egg in a measuring jug, make up to ½ pint with water; beat well with a fork. Place flour in a basin, gradually blend in egg and water and mix until smooth.

4. Heat a little oil or lard in a 6in frying pan. Add about 2 tablespoons of the batter and fry until golden brown on one side only, then slide on to a board, cooked side downwards. Make 5 more pancakes. Turn pancakes over, divide filling between them and spread down centre of each pancake. Brush edges with remaining batter. Fold 2 edges in, then roll up, taking care not to stretch pancakes; press edges together to seal.

5. Heat a pan of oil or lard to 370 deg F or until a 1in cube of day-old bread browns in 40 seconds. Place the rolls in the frying basket. Lower gently into pan and fry for 5 minutes, until golden brown. Drain on kitchen paper; pile on a hot dish and serve.

Crispy Noodles

To make 6 coils:

6oz ribbon noodles   Oil or lard for deep frying

1. Cook noodles in boiling, salted water for 9 minutes, or as directed on carton. Drain and rinse with cold water.

2. Heat a pan of oil or lard to 370 deg F, or until a 1in cube of day-old bread browns in 40 seconds. Form noodles into 6 coils with a spoon and fork; place in a frying basket and fry for 2 minutes or until crisp and golden brown. Drain thoroughly on kitchen paper and pile on to a dish.

Sweet and Sour Fish

For 3 or 4 portions:

8oz long-grain rice
Half a green pepper
Boiling water
2 rounded teaspoons cornflour
2 level teaspoons castor sugar
3 level teaspoons tomato purée

1 tablespoon vinegar
2 teaspoons soy sauce
1 small (8oz) can crushed pineapple
Salt and pepper
1 pack (12) crispy cod fries

1. Cook rice, as directed on page 76.

2. Discard seeds, core and white pith from green pepper; slice pepper into strips. Cover with boiling water and leave for 10 minutes; drain.

3. Blend cornflour, sugar and ½ pint water together in a medium-sized saucepan. Add tomato purée, vinegar, soy sauce, green pepper and crushed pineapple. Bring to boil, stirring; cover and simmer for 10 minutes. Taste and season with some salt and pepper and add more vinegar, if necessary.

4. Cook crispy cod fries, as directed on pack.

5. Pile rice on to a warmed serving dish and arrange cod fries on top. Pour sauce over. Serve immediately.

Chicken Chow Mein

For 4 portions:

1 small onion
1 small green pepper
1 small red pepper
2 sticks of celery
4oz button mushrooms
8oz cooked chicken
1½oz butter or margarine
1oz cornflour

¾ pint chicken stock
1 level tablespoon soy sauce
1 level teaspoon salt
Pepper
8oz ribbon noodles
Knob of butter
Oil or lard for deep frying

1. Peel and chop onion. Cut peppers in halves lengthwise; discard seeds, core and white pith. Cut peppers into ¼in dice. Place in a small bowl, cover with boiling water and leave for 1 minute; drain.

2. Wash celery and mushrooms. Chop celery and slice mushrooms. Cut chicken into even-sized pieces.

3. Melt fat in a saucepan, add onion and fry until transparent. Add celery and mushrooms; cook for 2 minutes.

4. Stir in cornflour and cook for 1 minute. Gradually add stock, bring to boil, stirring, and cook for 1 minute. Add peppers, soy sauce, salt, some pepper and chicken; cover and simmer for 15 minutes, stirring occasionally.

5. Cook noodles in boiling, salted water for 9 minutes, or as directed on carton. Drain and rinse with hot water. Put one-third of noodles aside. Add butter to remaining noodles and toss. Turn out on to a serving dish. Cover with a plate or foil and keep hot in a warm oven.

6. To make crispy noodles: Heat a pan of oil or lard to 370 deg F, or until a 1in cube of day-old bread browns in

40 seconds. Divide remaining noodles into 4 and form into coils. Fry for 2 minutes or until crisp and golden brown; drain thoroughly on kitchen paper and pile on to a warmed dish.

7. Remove soft noodles from oven, pour chicken sauce over. Serve with crispy noodles.

Chicken with Almonds

For 4 portions:

4 chicken breast joints	2oz blanched almonds
1 medium-sized onion	1 level tablespoon cornflour
2in piece of cucumber	½ level teaspoon salt
Half a 10oz can water	Pinch of pepper
chestnuts	Pinch of ground ginger
1 (10oz) can bean sprouts	1 tablespoon soy sauce
2 tablespoons oil	8oz long-grain rice

1. Remove chicken meat from joints and cut into thin strips. (It is easier to remove meat from joints while they are still partially frozen.) Place bones and skin in a saucepan, cover with water and bring to boil; cover and simmer for 1 hour, then strain. Reserve stock.

2. Peel and chop onion, dice cucumber, slice chestnuts and drain bean sprouts.

3. Heat oil in a large frying pan, add almonds and fry until golden brown. Remove from pan and drain on kitchen paper.

4. Add onion and chicken to pan and fry over a high heat, until chicken turns white, about 5 minutes. Add cucumber, chestnuts and bean sprouts; cook, stirring, for 2 minutes.

5. Blend cornflour, salt, pepper, ginger and soy sauce together in a basin. Add ½ pint of the chicken stock and stir well. Add to pan and stir over a moderate heat until sauce boils. Simmer for 5 minutes.

6. Meanwhile, cook rice, as directed on page 76.

7. Arrange a border of rice on a warmed serving dish and place chicken mixture in centre. Sprinkle with almonds and serve immediately.

Beef with Green Pepper

Soy sauce and ginger are popular ingredients in Chinese cookery. Here, they give a delicious flavour to the steak.

For 4 portions:

¾ lb rump steak

MARINADE:

¼ level teaspoon	2 teaspoons soy sauce
bicarbonate of soda	1 level tablespoon cornflour
½ level teaspoon salt	6 tablespoons water
1 teaspoon vinegar	
	2 tablespoons oil
1 large green pepper	1 chicken stock cube
1 clove of garlic	½ pint boiling water
Salt	1 tablespoon cooking sherry
1 spring onion	
1 piece preserved stem	
ginger	

1. Remove any fat from steak and cut meat into strips, ½in wide and 2in long.

2. Place ingredients for marinade in a bowl; add 6 tablespoons water and mix well. Add steak and turn in marinade; leave for 15 minutes.

3. Cut pepper in half lengthwise; discard seeds, core and white pith. Cut pepper into strips and place in a small saucepan. Cover with cold water, bring to boil, then drain. Peel clove of garlic and place on a saucer with a little salt. Using a round-ended knife, rub salt against the garlic to crush clove. Remove root from spring onion; chop onion. Chop ginger.

4. Heat oil in a frying pan. Add green pepper, garlic, onion and ginger; cook for 1 minute. Add beef and marinade to pan and cook, stirring, for 2 minutes. Dissolve chicken stock cube in boiling water and add to pan, stirring; add sherry. Bring to boil, stirring, and cook for a further 5 to 6 minutes, until steak is tender. Taste and add more soy sauce, if necessary. Serve with boiled long-grain rice (see page 76).

Frickadel Djagung

(Sweet Corn Fritters)

In Indonesia, fresh kernels from corn on the cob are used.

Makes 8:

1 small onion	1 (½ lb) pack frozen sweet
1 clove of garlic	corn kernels, just thawed
Salt	2 level tablespoons
1 (4oz) packet frozen	plain flour
prawns, just thawed	Pepper
2 standard eggs	Oil

1. Peel and finely chop onion. Peel clove of garlic and place on a saucer with a little salt. Using a round-ended knife, rub salt against garlic to crush clove.

2. Chop prawns. Lightly beat eggs in a bowl. Add onion, garlic, prawns, sweet corn, flour and some salt and pepper; mix well.

3. Heat some oil in a large frying pan. Add sweet corn mixture in tablespoonsful to pan and fry for 5 to 6 minutes, until golden brown, turning once. Remove from pan and drain on crumpled kitchen paper. Serve immediately. This dish is suitable for a snack or high tea.

Indonesia

Nasi Goreng

1

3

2

4

Nasi Goreng means 'fried rice'. This very typical Indonesian dish is a great favourite in the Netherlands, too. Rice is the staple diet of Indonesia, and in some parts of the country is often served three times a day in various delicious ways. Indonesian food is generally highly seasoned with many of the spices grown in the country: the people of Sumatra, for example, like their food very hot and peppery, with chilli added. Very little meat is eaten, and a small quantity is made to go a long way by the addition of many sauces and side dishes. Pineapple, bananas, peanuts, fresh coconut and pickled or fresh cucumbers are used extensively in Indonesian cookery. For dessert, tapioca pudding, spicy fruit salad of sweet and sour fruits, and banana dishes are served.

ingredients

For 4 portions:
12oz long-grain rice
¼lb cooked ham
4oz fresh, frozen or canned prawns
1 chicken joint
½lb onions
1 clove of garlic
1 rounded teaspoon salt

4 tablespoons oil
1 level teaspoon curry powder
1oz butter

OMELET:
2 standard eggs
Salt and pepper
½oz butter

GARNISH:
6 prawns in shells (optional)

method

1. Cook rice in a large saucepan containing at least 3 pints of boiling, salted water for about 12 minutes. Test by pressing a grain between thumb and finger; drain and rinse with cold water. Dice ham. Drain prawns (if canned) and rinse with cold water. Discard skin from chicken joint; cut off meat and cut in pieces. Peel and slice onions. Peel clove of garlic and place on a saucer with salt. Using a round-ended knife, rub salt against the garlic to crush clove.

2. Heat oil in a large frying pan and fry onion rings for 3 minutes without browning. Reserve a few for garnish and keep on a plate. Add garlic, curry powder and chicken to pan and cook, stirring continuously, for 5 minutes. Add cooked rice, 1oz butter, ham and prawns; heat through.

3. Beat eggs, 2 tablespoons water and some salt and pepper together in a basin. Heat ½oz of butter slowly in an 8in frying pan. Swirl to coat pan, then pour in egg mixture. Keep heat under pan fairly high. When brown underneath, flip over with a palette knife or fish slice; press down and cook until brown on the other side.

4. Turn out on to a board and cut into ½in-wide strips. To serve: Pile rice mixture on a serving dish and arrange strips on top in a lattice pattern. Arrange reserved onion rings and prawns in shells, if used, around edge. Serve with green and red pepper salad, sliced pickled or fresh cucumber and prawn crackers.

Sate

Traditionally Sate is grilled on small bamboo skewers. Other meats such as lamb, veal and chicken can be used. Chicken Sate should be served with peanut sauce (see recipe).

For 4 portions:

1lb rump steak	*½ level teaspoon garlic salt*
1 medium-sized onion	*1 tablespoon oil*
1 small green pepper	*1 level teaspoon granulated*
3 tablespoons lemon juice	*sugar*
3 tablespoons soy sauce	

1. Trim steak, if necessary, and cut into 1in dice. Peel and finely chop onion. Cut pepper in half lengthwise; remove seeds, core and white pith. Chop pepper and place with onion in a bowl.

2. Add lemon juice, soy sauce, garlic salt, oil and sugar, and mix together. Add steak and turn in mixture; leave for 15 minutes.

3. Remove rack from grill pan and prepare a moderate grill. Lift out steak, reserving soy sauce mixture, and thread on to 4 or 6 skewers, depending on size. Arrange in grill pan, pour soy sauce mixture over and grill for 10 to 15 minutes, turning skewers occasionally and basting with mixture, until steak is tender.

4. Remove skewers, place on a serving dish and keep hot. Cook sauce mixture in grill pan under moderate heat for 2 to 3 minutes, stirring occasionally. Pour into a small sauceboat.

5. Serve sate with boiled long-grain rice (see page 76) and sauce.

Gado Gado

(Cooked Salad)

In Indonesia far less meat is eaten than in most other Oriental countries and vegetable dishes are frequently served with spicy sauces.

For 4 portions:

2 standard eggs	*½lb spinach*
Half a cucumber	*1 (10oz) can bean sprouts*
2 medium-sized potatoes	*1 medium-sized onion*
4 carrots	*1 tablespoon oil*
½lb French beans	*Peanut Sauce (see recipe)*

1. Hard boil eggs for 10 minutes, crack and leave in cold water to cool. Shell and dry on kitchen paper; cut into slices. Wash and slice cucumber.

2. Peel and thinly slice potatoes; peel or scrape carrots and thinly slice. Cook carrots in a medium-sized saucepan of boiling, salted water for 10 minutes. Add potatoes to pan and cook for a further 8 to 10 minutes, until potatoes and carrots are just tender; drain and keep hot.

3. Wash beans, trim each end and cut into 1in lengths. Cook in boiling, salted water for 15 minutes; drain and keep hot.

4. Wash spinach thoroughly, removing all coarse stalks. Place in a saucepan with just enough water to cover base of saucepan; cover and cook over moderate heat for 10 to 12 minutes, or until tender. Drain spinach in a sieve and press to remove excess water; keep hot.

5. Place contents of can of bean sprouts in a saucepan and heat through; drain and keep hot. Peel and slice onion. Heat oil in a frying pan, add onion and fry until golden brown.

6. Layer all vegetables, except onions, in a warmed 3-pint casserole. Cover with hard-boiled eggs. Pour hot Peanut Sauce over and top with fried onions. Serve hot.

Peanut Sauce

A delicious, spicy sauce, which is served with Gado Gado and Chicken Sate.

1 small onion	*4 level tablespoons peanut*
1 clove of garlic	*butter*
Salt	*½ level teaspoon chilli*
4 tablespoons desiccated	*powder*
coconut	*1 level teaspoon soft brown*
½ pint boiling water	*sugar*
1 tablespoon oil	*1 bay leaf*
Juice of ½ lemon	

1. Peel and finely chop onion. Peel clove of garlic and place on a saucer with a little salt. Using a round-ended knife, rub salt against the garlic to crush clove.

2. Place coconut in a jug and add boiling water. Leave for 15 minutes, then strain in a sieve, reserving liquor, pressing until all liquid is removed from coconut.

3. Heat oil in a saucepan. Add onion and garlic and fry until onion is tender. Stir in coconut liquor, lemon juice, peanut butter, chilli powder, sugar and bay leaf. Bring to boil, stirring; cover and simmer for 10 to 15 minutes, until sauce has thickened. Taste and add more salt, if necessary. Remove bay leaf and serve sauce hot.

Banana Cake

4oz margarine	*A few drops vanilla*
10oz castor sugar	*essence*
2 standard eggs	*10oz self-raising flour*
10oz peeled bananas,	
about 4 small ripe	
bananas	

1. Prepare a cool oven (325 deg F, Gas Mark 3). Grease a 2lb loaf tin and line base with greaseproof paper; grease paper.

2. Cream margarine and sugar together until light and fluffy. Beat eggs and add gradually, beating well after each addition.

3. Slice bananas; mash lightly with a fork. Fold into creamed mixture with vanilla essence and flour.

4. Turn mixture into tin; smooth top. Bake in centre of oven for 2 hours, until risen and golden brown. Test by pressing with the fingers. If cooked, cake should spring back, have stopped bubbling and have begun to shrink from sides of tin. Leave in tin for 30 minutes; turn out and leave to cool completely on a wire rack.

The Cooking of North America

The cooking of the United States and Canada has a long tradition: it originates from the Indian tribes and some American dishes still bear their original Indian names. The native corn (sweet corn) is used in a variety of ways and is also ground to make cornmeal. American cookery is also influenced by the cookery of European immigrants. Most people, when thinking of American food, conjure up visions of huge juicy steaks and those rich, melt-in-the-mouth cakes covered with marshmallow-like frosting, which Americans offer their guests with a cup of delicious coffee in the evenings: Devil's Food Cake is just such a cake. Also typical of North American cooking are pies, both sweet and savoury, usually made in a pie plate, with pastry top and bottom. In this chapter, you'll find other tempting recipes adapted, in some cases, for use with British ingredients.

Canada

Tourtière

1

2

3

4

Tourtière is a well known Canadian meat pie; it comes from Quebec and is traditionally served after midnight mass at Christmas. The pork filling is mildly and deliciously spiced with cloves.

ingredients

For 4 or 5 portions:
FILLING:
5 rashers streaky bacon
1 medium-sized onion
1 medium-sized potato
1lb lean pie pork
1 clove of garlic
1 level teaspoon salt
¼ level teaspoon pepper

Pinch of ground cloves
Pinch of mixed dried herbs
2 rounded tablespoons
plain flour

SHORTCRUST PASTRY:
10oz plain flour
½ level teaspoon salt
2½oz lard
2½oz margarine
Cold water to mix
Beaten egg or milk to glaze

method

1. Remove rind and bone from bacon; peel and cut onion and potato into strips. Cut pork into strips. Finely mince bacon, onion, potato and pork. Peel clove of garlic and place on a saucer with salt. Using a round-ended knife, rub salt against the garlic to crush clove. Place minced meat and vegetables, garlic, pepper, cloves, herbs and flour in a saucepan. Add

½ pint water and bring to boil, stirring. Reduce heat to low, cover and simmer for 35 minutes, stirring occasionally. Remove from heat and cool meat quickly, by placing saucepan in cold water.

2. Prepare a moderately hot oven (400 deg F, Gas Mark 6). Place flour and salt in a bowl; add fats, cut into small pieces, and rub in with the fingertips until mixture resembles fine breadcrumbs. Mix in about 3 tablespoons cold water and mix to form a firm dough. Turn out on to a floured board and knead lightly. Cut off one-third of dough; roll out remaining piece to a round, 3in larger than an 8½in oven-glass pie plate. Roll pastry around rolling pin and lift on to pie plate. Gently ease pastry into pie plate and press into corners. Trim off edge, holding pie plate in left hand, and knife at an angle away from pie plate.

3. Place cooled meat filling in pie plate. Roll out remaining pastry to a circle, 1in larger than top of pie plate. Brush pastry rim with beaten egg or milk, place pastry lid on top and press edges together, to seal firmly.

4. Trim edges and cut with back of a knife to form flakes. Flute edge, by pressing out lightly with thumb and pulling in with the back of a round-ended knife. Make a hole in centre of pie, to allow steam to escape; brush pie with beaten egg or milk. Roll out pastry trimmings and cut into 'leaves'; arrange around centre hole. Brush leaves with beaten egg or milk and cook pie in centre of oven for 40 to 45 minutes. Serve hot with vegetables or cold with a green salad.

Brunswick Stew

This is a famous dish from the Southern States. It is often made in large quantities for out-of-doors parties; rabbit can be used in place of chicken.

For 4 to 6 portions:

4 large chicken joints
½ pint boiling water
Salt
1 medium-sized onion
3 medium-sized potatoes
1 large (14oz) can peeled tomatoes
1 (½lb) pack frozen broad beans

2 level teaspoons castor sugar
1 small (7oz) can sweet corn kernels
2 level tablespoons cornflour
Pepper

1. Place chicken joints in a large saucepan; add the boiling water and 2 level teaspoons salt. Bring to boil, cover and simmer for 35 minutes.

2. Peel and thinly slice onion and potatoes.

3. Lift chicken from stock; leave to cool. Remove chicken meat from bones; discard bones and skin. Cut meat in pieces.

4. Return chicken to stock in saucepan with onion, potatoes, contents of can of tomatoes, broad beans and sugar. Bring to boil, cover and simmer until potatoes and onion are cooked, about 30 minutes. Add contents of can of corn. Blend cornflour with a little water and stir into stew. Taste and season with some salt and pepper; simmer for 5 minutes. Serve hot.

Chicken Maryland

For 4 portions:

Oil or lard for deep frying
2 standard eggs
4 chicken joints
Fresh white breadcrumbs
4oz plain flour

¼ pint milk
Salt and pepper
1 small (¼lb) pack frozen sweet corn kernels
4 bananas

1. Heat a pan of oil or lard to 370 deg F, or until a 1in cube of day-old bread browns in 40 seconds.

2. Beat 1 egg with a fork; coat chicken joints with egg, then with breadcrumbs. Cook in frying basket in oil or lard for 15 to 20 minutes, depending on size.

3. Separate remaining egg. Place flour in a bowl, add egg yolk, milk and some salt and pepper; beat until smooth. Stir in sweet corn. Whisk egg white until stiff; fold into batter.

4. When chicken is cooked, place on kitchen paper on a dish, to drain; keep warm.

5. Peel bananas and fry in the hot fat until pale golden brown; keep hot.

6. Drop dessertspoonsful of corn batter into the hot fat and fry, until golden brown and puffed up.

7. Arrange chicken joints, corn fritters and bananas on a warmed serving dish. Serve with a green salad.

Potatoes with Chive and Soured Cream Dressing

For 4 portions:

4 large potatoes
1 (5 fluid oz) carton soured cream

1 rounded tablespoon chopped chives
Salt and pepper

1. Prepare a moderate oven (350 deg F, Gas Mark 4).

2. Wash and scrub potatoes and remove any eyes; prick potatoes all over.

3. Place potatoes on a baking sheet in oven and cook for 1 to 1½ hours, or until soft.

4. Mix soured cream and chives together and season with some salt and pepper.

5. When potatoes are cooked, make a cut in top of each potato; press gently at base to open. Serve immediately with dressing.

Note: If soured cream is not available, stir 1 teaspoon lemon juice into 5 fluid oz single cream.

Kentucky Cheesecake

Cheesecake was taken to North America by German and Austrian immigrants. Over the years, it has changed from the Continental type of cheesecake (see recipe on page 49) to a richer variety, usually with a biscuit-crumb base, that is typically American. Sometimes, canned fruit is arranged on the top of the cheesecake and glazed.

For 8 portions:

6oz digestive biscuits
3oz butter
3oz soft brown sugar
½ level teaspoon ground cinnamon
8oz cream cheese
4oz curd cheese

2 standard eggs
4oz castor sugar
2 level tablespoons cornflour
½ teaspoon vanilla essence
1 (5 fluid oz) carton soured cream

1. Prepare a moderate oven (350 deg F, Gas Mark 4). Brush a 7in, loose-based, deep round cake tin with a little melted butter.

2. Crush biscuits between 2 sheets of greaseproof paper, using a rolling pin.

3. Melt butter in a saucepan, remove from heat and mix in brown sugar, crushed biscuits and cinnamon; mix well. Reserve 3 rounded tablespoons of the crumb mixture; press remainder firmly into base of tin.

4. Place cheeses in a basin. Separate eggs; place whites in a clean, grease-free bowl. Add yolks to cheese with castor sugar, cornflour and vanilla essence; mix well.

5. Whisk egg whites until stiff, but not dry. Fold into cheese mixture with half the soured cream. Turn into tin and level top with back of spoon.

6. Place on a baking sheet and bake in centre of oven for 1 hour, until well risen and golden brown on top. Spread remaining soured cream over top and sprinkle with reserved crumbs. Leave to cool in tin (cheesecake will slowly sink in centre). When quite cold, place tin centrally on a 1lb-size can and gently pull down side of tin. Loosen cheesecake from base with a knife and slide on to a serving dish.

Note: If soured cream is not available, stir 1 teaspoon lemon juice into 5 fluid oz single cream.

Pancakes

These light, tender pancakes are much thicker than their English counterparts. The secret of making them successfully is to mix the batter very lightly; do not beat it until it is smooth. We substituted yoghourt for the buttermilk used in the traditional American recipe.

For 3 portions:
PANCAKES:

1oz butter
2 level tablespoons golden syrup
1 standard egg
1 (5 fluid oz) carton natural yoghourt

1 level teaspoon bicarbonate of soda
4 tablespoons milk
4oz plain flour

TOPPING:
Butter
Warmed golden or maple syrup

1. Place 1oz butter in a small saucepan. Measure syrup carefully, levelling off spoon with a knife and making sure there is none on underside of spoon; add to butter. Stir over a low heat until butter has melted.

2. Beat egg and yoghourt together. Dissolve bicarbonate of soda in the milk and add to yoghourt mixture with flour; mix lightly (the batter should not be completely smooth).

3. Lightly grease a large, thick-based frying pan; place over a moderate heat. Test heat of frying pan; a drop of water should just sizzle when dropped in pan.

4. Drop tablespoonsful of batter into pan; cook until bubbles begin to burst on top, and pancakes are golden brown on underside. Turn over with a fish slice and cook until golden brown on other side, about 3 minutes. Place on a warmed dish, cover with a lid or foil and keep warm while cooking remaining batter, to make a total of 12 pancakes.

5. To serve: Pile pancakes, 4 on each plate, with a knob of butter between each pancake. Serve with warmed golden or maple syrup.

Angel Food Cake

This famous cake from America is traditionally made in a tall ring tin, 10in in diameter. We reduced ingredients to enable the cake to be cooked in our more readily-available ring mould. It's pure white inside with a very light texture.

2oz plain flour
3oz castor sugar
4 standard egg whites

1 level teaspoon cream of tartar
½ teaspoon vanilla essence

FROSTING:
3oz plain chocolate
2oz butter

1 standard egg yolk
4oz icing sugar

1. Prepare a cool oven (325 deg F, Gas Mark 3). Dust a 1½-pint capacity plain ring mould with a little flour.

2. Sift flour and sugar together; repeat.

3. Place egg whites in a clean, grease-free bowl, add cream of tartar and whisk until stiff, but not dry. Whisk in vanilla essence.

4. Fold in flour mixture lightly, but thoroughly, cutting through mixture with a metal spoon. Spoon into mould; cut through mixture with a knife to disperse any large air bubbles, then level top.

5. Bake in centre of oven for 45 minutes. Test by pressing with the fingers. If cooked, cake should feel firm, have turned a pale golden brown on top and have begun to shrink from sides of mould.

6. Invert mould on a jar or bottle and leave to become quite cold. Ease cake out of mould with a palette knife.

7. To make frosting: Break up chocolate; place in a basin over a saucepan of hot, but not boiling, water. Add butter and stir until melted. Beat egg yolk and 1 dessertspoon water together and stir into chocolate. Remove from heat and stir in icing sugar. Beat with a wooden spoon until thick enough to spread; spread over cake and swirl with a round-ended knife.

America

Devil's Food Cake

2

1

3

4

It is not possible to make exactly the same type of soft, fluffy, American cake in this country, because of the different flour available. This is the reason why it is often difficult to get a good result when using a recipe from an American cook book. Our recipe, with its easy method and large amount of raising agent, gives the nearest texture possible to an American cake.

ingredients

CAKE:

2oz cocoa
6 tablespoons boiling water
6oz soft margarine
6oz castor sugar
4 standard eggs
6oz self-raising flour
2 level teaspoons baking powder

FILLING:

1oz plain chocolate
6oz icing sugar
2oz butter or margarine
1 tablespoon milk

FROSTING:

12oz castor sugar
2 egg whites
4 tablespoons hot water
Pinch of cream of tartar

method

1. Prepare a cool oven (325 deg F, Gas Mark 3). Brush 2 (7in) or 2 (8in) sandwich tins with oil or melted fat and line each with a circle of greaseproof paper; grease paper. Place cocoa in a basin and add boiling water. Mix well and place in a large mixing bowl, together with margarine, sugar, eggs, flour and baking powder. Beat with a wooden spoon for 1 to 2 minutes, until mixture is well blended. (For economy, replace 1 egg with 2 egg yolks and save whites for frosting.)

2. Either divide mixture into 3 and spread one-third into each 7in tin, reserving one-third, or divide mixture into half and spread in 2 (8in) tins. Bake just above centre of oven for 35 to 40 minutes. Test by pressing with the fingers. If cooked, cakes should spring back, have stopped bubbling and have begun to shrink from sides of tins. Leave in tins for 5 minutes, then turn out, remove paper and place on a wire rack to cool thoroughly. (If using 7in tins, wash one and use, as before, to bake remaining mixture.) To make filling: Break chocolate into small pieces. Place in a basin over a saucepan of hot, but not boiling, water; leave to melt, giving an occasional stir. Sieve icing sugar. Beat butter or margarine and half the icing sugar together until light and fluffy. Mix in melted chocolate and remainder of icing sugar, add milk and beat until smooth. Sandwich cakes together with filling. Place cake on a cake stand or serving dish.

3. To make frosting: Bring a saucepan of water to boil and remove from heat. Place all ingredients in a clean, grease-free bowl over saucepan. Whisk at high speed with an electric whisk for about 5 minutes, or with a rotary whisk for about 10 minutes, until mixture stands in soft peaks on whisk.

4. Pour over cake and spread over side with a palette knife. Mark vertical lines in frosting around side and make 5 swirls on top of cake; leave to set.

Note: Cake may be made in advance, but frost the cake on the day it is required. Store in a tin, not an air-tight plastic container.

Applesauce Muffins

Muffins are to Americans are as scones are to the British. They may be flavoured in a variety of ways, but the essence of a really light muffin is to mix the batter just enough to incorporate the liquid.

Makes 12 or 18:

6oz plain flour	2oz lard
2 level teaspoons baking powder	3oz soft brown sugar
½ level teaspoon bicarbonate of soda	2oz seedless raisins
½ to 1 level teaspoon cinnamon	1 standard egg
¼ level teaspoon mixed spice	1 small (4½oz) can baby food strained apples
	¼ pint milk

1. Prepare a moderately hot oven (400 deg F, Gas Mark 6). Grease 12 deep, individual Yorkshire-pudding tins or 18 tartlet tins.

2. Sift flour, baking powder, bicarbonate of soda, cinnamon and mixed spice into a bowl. Add lard, cut into small pieces, and rub in with the fingertips until mixture resembles fine breadcrumbs. Mix in sugar and raisins.

3. Beat egg, apple and milk together. Add to flour mixture and mix quickly with a fork. (The batter should have a fairly lumpy consistency.)

4. Divide mixture between the tins and bake just above centre of oven for 20 to 25 minutes.

5. Remove from tins and serve hot with butter.

Divinity Candy

These delicious sweets are a great favourite in North America. No candy stall at a sale of work or bazaar is complete without these famous home-made confections, rather like our own national favourite, fudge.

Makes about 30 candies:

2oz glacé cherries	3oz golden syrup
2oz walnuts	1 egg white
½oz angelica (optional)	½ teaspoon vanilla essence
8oz granulated sugar	

1. Place a sheet of greaseproof paper on a baking sheet and brush with oil or melted fat.

2. Chop cherries, walnuts and angelica, if used, finely.

3. Place sugar, syrup and ¼ pint water in a medium-sized, heavy-based saucepan. Stir over a moderate heat until sugar has dissolved. Bring to boil and cook, without stirring, for 7 to 10 minutes, until 'hard ball' stage is reached (250 deg F on a sugar thermometer, or until a little syrup, when dropped into a saucer of cold water, forms a firm ball).

4. Meanwhile, place egg white in a clean, grease-free bowl and whisk until stiff, but not dry.

5. Pour syrup, in a thin stream, on to egg white, while whisking with an electric mixer or wire whisk. Whisk until mixture thickens and lightens in colour. Whisk in vanilla essence. Continue whisking until mixture will hold its shape.

6. Quickly mix in cherries, nuts and angelica.

7. Drop teaspoonsful of mixture on to greaseproof paper and leave to set.

Baked Alaska

For 6 portions:
SPONGE BASE:

1 standard egg and 2 egg yolks	2oz castor sugar
	2oz self-raising flour

MERINGUE TOPPING:

2 egg whites	1 family-size brick ice cream (any flavour)
3oz castor sugar	

1. Prepare a moderately hot oven (400 deg F, Gas Mark 6). Brush a shallow 7in square tin with melted fat and line the base with greaseproof paper; grease paper.

2. Bring a saucepan of water to the boil and remove from heat. Place egg, egg yolks and 2oz sugar in a bowl over saucepan and whisk until mixture becomes thick and leaves a trail when whisk is lifted. Remove from heat and continue whisking until mixture is cool. Sift flour and gently fold into egg mixture with a metal spoon. Pour into tin and bake in centre of oven for about 15 minutes. Test by pressing with the fingers. If cooked, cake should spring back, have stopped bubbling and have begun to shrink from sides of tin. Turn out and remove paper; leave to cool on a wire rack.

3. Increase oven temperature to very hot (475 deg F, Gas Mark 9).

4. Trim sponge to fit ice cream brick (the trimmings of sponge can be used for a trifle).

5. Place egg whites in a clean, grease-free bowl and whisk until stiff, but not dry. Whisk in half the sugar, then fold in remainder with a metal spoon.

6. Place sponge on an ovenproof plate and place ice cream brick on top.

7. Completely cover ice cream and sponge with meringue and mark swirls or peaks with a spoon.

8. Bake for 2 to 3 minutes in centre of oven until meringue is golden brown. Serve immediately.

Note: The sponge base may be prepared in advance. Egg whites will keep for 2 to 3 days in a covered container in the refrigerator.

Foreign Index

English Index

First Published in 1970 by FAMILY CIRCLE,
Elm House, Elm Street, London, WC1. Printed in Italy by ILTE.
1970 © Standbrook Publications Ltd, a Member of The Thomson Organisation Ltd